This book is dedicated
a great Master Chef, and to my son,
who has inherited not only his grandfather's
name, but, I hope, also his qualities.

Carmelo Sammarco

SICILIAN COOKING

Typical Sicilian recipes

INTRODUCTION BY ELDA JOLY
INK DRAWINGS BY RODO SANTORO

ARNONE Editore - Palermo

The recipes are easy and, I hope, clear. But I feel that just one or two things need pointing out, especially for the non-Sicilian readers amongst you (and the cooks of course!).

If you can't lay your hands on all the ingredients you need for the recipes in the area where you live, my suggestion is that you stock up here in Sicily at the traditional markets, like "la Vucciria" in Palermo for example. Ask the shopkeeper about the best way of preserving products.

"Passolina", for example, is a type of small, black raisin, not as sweet as ordinary ones, but there is no substitute for them; if you can't get any, it's better to do without them.

With regards to fresh ingredients, which obviously wouldn't stand up to the journey, you could try using similar items found locally, after having tasted the dishes here in Sicily. You can substitute fresh caciocavallo cheese for instance, with any other kind of equally matured cow's milk cheese. But I honestly don't know what you could use in place of "tenerumi", which are the freshest, most tender leaves from a kind of courgette ("zucchina lunga") which only grows locally. I have tried however to keep these instances down to a minimum.

One last thing. In Sicily both "mollica" and "pangrattato" mean stale grated bread (breadcrumbs), whereas in other parts of Italy there is a difference in that "mollica" is made only from the soft part of the bread and not the crust. In the recipes I've used breadcrumbs for both terms, but surely I'm allowed one little indulgence, aren't I? Or would you rather prefer the recipes were written in Sicilian dialect? Enjoy your meal!

Carmelo Sammarco

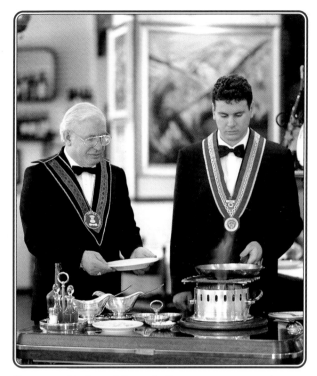

Francesco Paolo and Carmelo Sammarco

Anna Sammarco

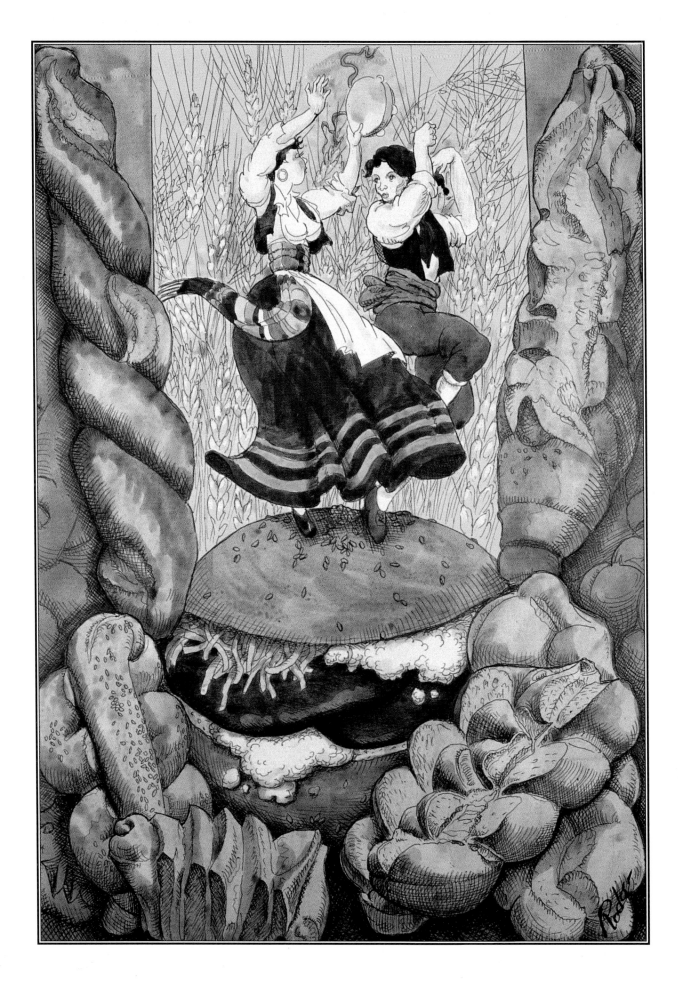

A LOOK AT SICILIAN COOKING

In the big tidy kitchens of the monastery, under the watchful eye of the head spice-man, the most important person among the monks, a swarm of lay sisters, novices and servants are pottering about amongst big wooden spoons and pots. Some of them are chopping away on boards, some are crushing with pestles and mortars and others are carefully mixing various ingredients and taking down precious, colourful bottles and decanters and jars full of jams, and stewed and syrupy fruits from the ventilated shelves amongst the shadows.

They are waiting for His Eminence and, forgetting, for a while, about the capital sins and the mortification of the flesh, they are preparing a cake, the pride of the convent, whose recipe has been passed down with the utmost secrecy: "the triumph of gluttony".

Little remains of this fascinating, mysterious, multicoloured and tasty cake except the name. I have thought about it while writing this introduction because it summarises the main characteristics of Sicilian cooking. These characteristics include the spectacular presentation of the dish on the table. This effect was achieved by both the abundance of the food itself and the pyramid type layout. This was the outcome of the formal exaltation of cooking, which must be re-assessed so that we do not forget what the rich Sicilian land has given us over time, both during the good times and the dark days alike.

* * *

In recent years, Sicilian cities, as elsewhere in the rest of Europe, have seen the opening of fast food joints. Here, where cooking habits still retain all the significance of a glorious tradition, the reactions have been varied.

The conservative types call it vulgar and irresponsible consumerism. "Disgraceful behaviour", cry those who look back fondly on the days of the soft, peaceful cafés, tea-rooms and pastry-shops, where the intellectuals hung out,

and on a Palermo famous for its vermouth at 11 and tea or an ice cream at 6... "Oh, how times change!".

However, if we really think about it, fast food has always been part of life in Palermo. In the old days, you could find it in the fried-food stalls which stood out in the big markets or hidden away in the alleys and back streets of the old city amongst its characteristic mix of smells, voices and colours. The fast food was carried about in baskets and bread bins by street sellers, calling out to possible customers as they walked through the streets.

The fast food was targeted at a clearly identified class of workers. It was aimed at those who were looking for a fast, cheap and tasty meal, which could be eaten on the streets, in the shade in summer, and in the sun in winter, during the daily work-break. In addition, there was no need to lay the table. This was replaced by the hot crispy bread with all sorts of delights: croquettes *(cazzilli)*, scraps, fried aubergine and spleen browned in lard, as an alternative to the big slices of soft bread topped with tomato, onion, anchovy and breadcrumb sauce *(u sfinciuni)*. All of this was washed down, not with wine, which was too expensive, but with water, often juiced up with a dash of lemon or with a few drops of a distillate of aniseed *(u zammu)*. In "happy" Palermo, this was the food of the workers, those who passed quickly from childhood to maturity, with a difficult life full of struggles and constantly oppressed by local or foreign masters, who followed one another and changed with the passing of time.

The more fortunate, with a bit more money to spend, were able to kill their hunger in the taverns where, along with the wine, they served hot, strongly spiced snacks to increase the thirst and, of course, the consumption of drinks. You did not order here: without any fuss, the barman prepared the dish of the day. It was a big dish, smelled nice and looked good. Indeed, satis-

fying the senses of smell, sight and taste was a source of well being and a real cure for the physical pains and the struggles of daily life.

All the others ate at home where a legion of "household angels" (grandmothers, mothers, aunts, wives and sisters, assisted by helpers and servants), spent entire mornings among pots and pans preparing succulent lunches for their masters and men.

Experts in Sicilian cooking discuss on the various types of dishes and identify two main lines: the simple food of the poor and the food of the aristocracy and upper-middle classes, the pride of *monsu* (top class cooks). These haughty cooks used to boss around a small group of apprentices, who were guilty of making mistakes in the daily recital of the manual of Artusi, waiving their rolling pins at them. This distinction is pure speculation. The reality is much more complex. As the old proverb goes: "tell me how you eat and I will tell you what you are".

Cooking can be considered the most fleeting of the arts. Still, it is strongly related to history, to tradition and, why not, to current fashion. In short, it is related to taste in the broadest meaning of the word.

Much has been written about Sicilian cooking. Doubts have been raised about the origin of sauces and dishes which reflect the nature and the inheritance of the various peoples who have inhabited the island. Without doubt, this has some truth to it. However, it is more realistic to consider Sicily's central position in the Mediterranean region. From the times of prehistory, this sea has united rather than divided its surrounding countries.

It is not easy to characterise Sicily. It is a place of violent passions, agonising melancholy and incredible contrasts. It is a microcosm which presents, in miniature form, all the components of a continent with a sufficiently mild climate, which changes as we move inland from the coast.

It has the most varied colours, enlivened by the sun. This explains all the various hues of blue of the sky and the sea, the various hues of green of the fields and the woods and the various dazzling whites, yellows and reds of the flowers. The crops have always been diversified and, to a certain degree, extended. First, we have a mature fruit near the coast, then in the hills and, finally, in the mountains.

For a land where agriculture was the dominating activity, this is particularly important. All kinds of plants take root and prosper without problems.

Surrounded by such bountiful nature, the Sicilian loves colours. Grey skies, lead-coloured seas and flat landscapes oppress and upset him, as if they were physical and moral ills.

Colour means joy, it means party-time, it means happiness. As we will see later, the cake, symbol of the party, is a celebration of colours, to feast with the eyes before the palate. It does not matter where these colours come from. What matters is that the table is always very rich. This explains the recent fortune of the kiwi fruit, an Australian fruit which is not especially tasty but is of an intense, brilliant green, animated by white and with small black rays. This is the same green which we find in a less intense form in the imitation fresh fruit, made with marzipan to a recipe which has varied little from ancient times as it has been passed down through the ages. The Romans, in particular, loved the produce of the island, especially Hyblaean honey, and they had a high opinion of the expertise of Sicilian cooks.

Sicilians also owe most of their spices, not to the Arabs, but to antiquity. These spices, together with the aromatic herbs, fill the island and give Sicilian cooking mysterious smells and tastes, with a vaguely Oriental feel. Dill, absinthe, juniper, garlic, onion, cloves, ginger, basil, pepper, cinnamon, cassia, cardamom, cumin, cinnamomum, coriander, fennel, laurel, lentiscus, sweet marjoram, oregano, mint, lavender, nutmeg, rosemary, rocket salad, sage, celery, saffron. All of these spices are listed in

the archives of Alexandria of Egypt, a type of fixed price, which dates back to the 4th century AD.

The spices, many of which had medicinal properties, were used to preserve as well as flavour the dishes. They flavoured sauces made with honey and vinegar which dress roasted or boiled vegetables, meat and fish, which date back to Roman times. This is documented by *Apicio*, gourmet and connoisseur of the 1st century AD.

Before the cities had large squalid public lodging areas, the people lived together in the suburbs and in the city centre. The noble palaces, the town houses and humble cottages had open balconies and terraces *(astrachi)*, where you found geraniums and begonias amongst the basil and mint. They tried to recreate the country, the green which is always present in the heart of the people. These terraces were like a multicoloured backdrop for the streets and courtyards. The impression was a vast, ever-changing stage representing the tragi-comedy of man.

Religious or civil feasts, family occasions: baptisms, weddings, funerals - any event was an excuse to prepare eloquent meals following an age-old menu with precise rituals: no meal worth its name had less than fifteen courses.

To start with, a consommé was more than sufficient to warm up the stomach. This was followed by the first courses (usually a very elaborate pasta). The second courses, meat and fish, were alternated with middle dishes and other delights, such as charcuteries, cheese, crushed olives, pickles, sun-dried tomatoes and whatever else was available!

The middle dishes came in all kinds of varieties: omelettes with vegetables, cheese and vegetable pies (aubergines, tomatoes, peppers, courgettes), filled and drowned in spicy or sweet sauces. However, the main middle dish was the so-called "mixed fry". "A meal without a fry is not a meal", according to those in the know.

Croquettes - rice, potato, semolina, milk, cream -, sliced cheeses, brain, spinal marrow, vegetables coated with breadcrumbs or with delicate batters followed one another in waves, hot and crispy, presented on large oblong trays adorned with fresh lettuce leaves.

With the passing of time and new cooking ideas, the abundant middle dishes, reduced in quantity, to make room for side dishes, gradually took on the role of starters and appetisers, not part of traditional Sicilian cuisine.

* * *

I have already pointed out that Sicilian cooking has two main lines, strictly related to the social class of the persons involved. Another difference must also be pointed out: the differences between the coastal areas and those inland, in the hills, if not in the mountains. In the Sicilian microcosm, distances are never excessive, especially nowadays when you can move from one end of the island to the other in a couple of hours.

If we go back in time, however, times become longer and a "trip" from Palermo-Catania, which now is a short trip by car, was a real journey, through changing landscapes and streets which were often in disorder, full of sharp rises and falls and sudden bends and turns. The journey required many days of riding on donkeys or mules or in one-horse carriages and carts.

* * *

Small rowing boats, vassals and hull and sail trawlers in a variety of colours unloaded their nets every day on the piers and in the creeks. Here they displayed their entire catch: fish, molluscs and crustaceans of all shapes and sizes, as well as the seasonal catch, be it swordfish or tuna fish.

The catch depended on the season but even more so on the sea in which the fish live and reproduce. The Strait of Messina, for example, is the area for catching swordfish. The Tyrrhenian Sea and, in part, the Sicilian Canal, provide blue fish: mackerel, sardines, anchovies, gurnards

and even white bream, dusky sea perch, soles and goatfish. The Ionian Sea provides molluscs and crustaceans, mussels and shellfish.

The Northern and Southern coasts, finally, were strewn with tuna nets where, in May and, to a lesser extent, in September, they performed the pagan tuna catching ritual, a tradition which dates back to the very earliest times. The tuna, once considered to be the meat of the poor, was processed and preserved in oil and salt.

The variety of the catch ensured that every coastal city could boast its own repertoire of recipes. The fish was almost never boiled (considered to be food for the sick). It was cooked whole or in slices together with molluscs and crustaceans in fragrant soups full of herbs and spices and flavoured with tomato or saffron, or roasted or fried. In this case, various sauces were added to bring out the taste.

The most common sauces were the simple *"sal-morigano"* (oil, lemon, oregano and garlic) and the more complex *"caponata"* (fried aubergines, capers, olives, celery, tomato, onion, sugar and vinegar). This is not to mention onions browned in a sweet and sour sauce, a mix of vinegar and sugar which was also used to preserve the dishes for more than a day when freezers and fridges were still not used.

Among the molluscs, the inhabitants of Palermo actually enjoyed octopus, boiled and seasoned with lemon, salt and pepper.

If common opinion attributes the invention of fish soups to the Aragonese or the treatment of stock fish to the international nature of Messina, everyone knows that fish *couscous*, a typical plate of Mazzara, Marsala and Trapani is a legacy of the Arab domination. However, we must ask ourselves why this is only common in a small part of the island. Fish *couscous*, in fact, is not very common in North Africa. In Tunisia, it is mainly eaten in the Sfax region as an alternative to meat (veal, mutton, chicken) *couscous*. It follows that the dish in Trapani may derive from a tradition which is more related to the continuous contact with mixed teams running

the tuna ritual. Surely, it is no coincidence that the head rower is known as *rais*! Nor must we forget that up to the last century, the Sicilian language was also spoken in the ports of Tunisia, even in the law courts.

In any case, fish, a basic foodstuff in the coastal areas, was difficult to bring to the central areas unless preserved in jars *(burnie)* in oil or salt.

* * *

But while it was difficult to bring the fresh fish to the populated centres in the middle of the island, at the time, processions *(retine)* of mules and carts brought the *meat* of the feuds to the city: legumes, vegetables and grains, *ricotta* and cheese, but mostly meat, usually slaughtered in the city, to be cooked with spices, aromatic herbs and vegetables. In reality, the pasture land was not very rich and the meats were not especially good. As well as bovine meat, a lot of mutton, pork and alternative meats (chicken, pigeon, rabbit, bred just about everywhere with little fuss) were eaten. All the meat, as well as being barbecued and fried, was slow cooked in earthenware pots with spices, aromas and vegetables which became full-bodied sauces whose fragrance filled the houses and the streets.

Those who had a shotgun could also count on non-migratory or migratory game, once very abundant. Hares, rabbit, skylarks, quails, thrushes, coots, mallards, wild boar, hedgehogs.

Everything which was wild and edible, suitably marinated, was another food resource. Still, meat was expensive. This justifies the variety of dishes in which meat was minced so that the hardest meat became soft and scraps and leftovers could be used. Treated in this way, the meat was used to fill timbales, pies and even vegetables: onions, aubergines, peppers and courgettes. It was also mixed with mashed potatoes or soaked bread to form meatballs which, fried or roasted, were added to sauces of every type and colour. This was a way to double the amount of food with the minimum of expense.

***

Sicilian cuisine has two undoubted sovereigns - when you don't want to consider them as guardian divinities - loved and venerated by everyone on the island: bread and pasta. It may be true that in recent times, their power has been threatened many times and they have been endlessly accused, sent to trial and abolished by supporters of the hard line. "You eat with bread", children used to be advised. Nowadays, pre-packaged snacks are preferred and, although they are guaranteed, they are not very wholesome. Our old sovereign, bread, was praised, sung about and revered during the Fascist period, especially during the time of the sanctions. We can consider bread to be a victim of political persecution that, sent into exile, was replaced by toasted bread, asphyxial breadsticks and *crackers*. A genuine Sicilian knows well that once you have left the Strait, it is better to make as little use of bread as possible. In this way, it takes on the aspect of a nostalgic memory.

Flour, water, and natural yeast. The dough, moulded into rounded or extended shapes (loafs, *pupe* and *picciriddi*) were lovingly wrapped in sheets of wool to help the leavening process and then cooked in earthenware and olive vine sarment ovens, red-hot from the flames. In the country areas, the dough was very compact. Bread was only made, in fact, a couple of times a month and the bread had to be edible for a very long time. Once it hardened, cooked with laurel, garlic and vegetable stock, it became a hot good-smelling soup. Fresh bread from the oven, with oil, oregano, salt, pepper, anchovies and a sprinkling of *pecorino*, was a choice dish.

In the city, bread was processed softer and white. Packed in various forms and enriched with sesame or poppy seeds, it was almost sweet. There was a distinction among strong bread, Spanish bread and French bread. The dough was different and they were eaten with different kinds of meals. Finally, small loafs (*muffulette* and *guastedde*) filled with chopped meat or ricotta and cheese or ricotta cream, candied fruit and chocolate *(iris)* turned the bread into a complete meal.

* * *

Some say it came to Sicily from China after the travels of Marco Polo. Others say that it has always existed on the island. The other sovereign, pasta, after a period of being neglected, if not actually ignored, returned to its rightful place in the kitchen as a result of the discovery of the Mediterranean diet. In truth, the Sicilians, from the coast to the mountains, have always regarded it highly, as a pillar of their cuisine.

From its earliest forms, prepared by hand: *tagliolini* (thin noodles), *quadrucci* (square noodles), *anelletti* (rings), *cavateddi* and *busi* (holed shaped pasta), with the arrival of pasta-making machines, a series of shapes has been developed for which there are two main lines: long pasta, to be wrapped around the fork and short pasta. Every pasta shape requires a special type of sauce.

Sumptuously wrapped in sweet or hot crusts or covered with a thin layer of breadcrumbs, with a sauce or in soup, pasta reigns over a nutritious team of handmaids and pageboys: the sauces. Nowadays, it is difficult to think that they had to do without tomato, as the image of spaghetti is commonly linked to tomato and basil sauce. We must remember that we cannot be sure that we owe the discovery of this vegetable to Christopher Columbus, given that some scholars identify in the tomato the famous fruits of the Hesperides related to the tale of Hercules. In any case, returning to the sauces, they range from the most simple garlic, oil and chilli pepper and its variants (with parsley, anchovies and toasted breadcrumbs) to elaborate sauces including all kinds of vegetables and legumes boiled or browned with aromatic herbs: healthy, tasty seasonings. Other sauces include: cheese *(tozzo)*, ricotta with fried courgettes and aubergines, as well as a number of soups with fish, shellfish, seafood, chopped meat and giblets. To summa-

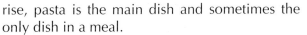

rise, pasta is the main dish and sometimes the only dish in a meal.

Rice was eaten less frequently. Imported from the East, perhaps from the Arabs, it passed through the island, leaving few but tasty reminders (timbales, rice patties, croquettes, sweet and hot pancakes, creamed rice and sweet rice ice cream) and then moved on to areas which are more suitable for its cultivation.

As for sweet corn, which came from the West Indies, it was considered bran feed for chicken!

Every month, there are two or three obligatory religious or civil feasts in Sicily. If we add private parties: birthdays, Saint's days, etc., there is a considerable number of occasions. In any case, both public and private parties were a time for one or more family clans to get together.

Conversations were held in the parlours of the aristocrats (from the cavaliers to the princes, there were quite a few). Arts, trades and professions united the members of the various associations: the brotherhoods and sisterhoods. The less well-to-do socialised daily in the courtyards and the alleys. Dressed in the most elegant of clothes, this colourful representation of humanity, went about the streets adorned in colour and light, showing themselves off in the holiday "parade". After all, dressing up is also an essential part of the Sicilian spirit.

It was essential to interrupt the walks *(u passiu)* with a stop-off in the cafés, a sanctuary for one's thirst, bedecked with all kinds of cakes and desserts, in every shape and colour. The dessert was such a part of the celebration ritual that it ended up characterising it: for example, the *buccellato* (ring-shaped cake) represents Christmas; the *sfincie* (cream puffs) represent Saint Joseph's Day, the *cassata* represents Easter, the *cannolo* represents Carnival and marzipan fruit represents All Souls' Day. We must also consider that some ingredients, apart from jams and preserves, were only available in certain periods of the year. For example, ricotta (November to April), watermelon (June to August), citrus fruits (November to April), just to mention a few.

Sicilian pastries, as we have already said, are mostly very rich. They are very sweet, extremely colourful and a joy to be beheld. The colours, when they cannot be created with raw materials, are created with multicoloured icing sugar and chocolate. This is topped with candied fruit or marzipan fruits, or aniseed wrapped with coloured sugar, or cylinders and balls of sweetened flour in a variety of colours: yellow, green, blue, red *(mbriaculicchi* and *cannettiglie)* and silver and golden balls and tablets.

No small or large centre in Sicily worth its name is without one or more typical cakes or desserts. It is impossible to remember all of them. Here are a few examples: the *"aranciata"* from Modica; the *pignoccata* from Messina; the *"testa di turco"* (fried pastry with cream) from Castelbuono, cheese cakes from Polizzi, the *"ossa di morto"* from Sciacca and the *cassata* from Palermo, the latter needing absolutely no description at all. Common to the whole island, we have *pasticciotti* made from almond-flour, short pastry and sweetened bread paste, filled with jams, preserves and custard. Among these, we have the famous *"minni di virgini"* (virgins' breasts) in eternal memory of Saint Agatha, patron saint of Catania and co-patron saint of Palermo.

Even the most concise of summaries of Sicilian cakes and sweets must include at least a brief description of the methods for preserving fruit, cooking it with sugar or in spirit or julep. The latter produced tasty syrups to be served cold and diluted as thirst-quenching drinks in the summer heat as an alternative to fresh squeezed juices.

Mixed with fish glue, the fruit juices had the consistency of soft gelatine (coffee, mulberry, wild black cherry) or were consolidated with starch as in the melon gel, a typical product of Palermo, with a faint odour of jasmine.

Fruit juices, essences, even spices are essential ingredients in the preparation of crushed ice drinks *(granite)*, sorbets *(sorbetti)* and ice cream, other undoubted masterpieces of our cuisine. In

the past, when artificial ice had not yet been discovered, the winter snow was preserved in holes and cracks covered with straw and rags. Long rows of mules came down from the mountains, bringing the residual snow used to cool the liquids until they were solid. According to the solidity and the creaminess of the compound, there was a distinction among soft ice creams *(cremolate)*, crushed ice drinks *(granite)*, sorbets *(sorbetti)* and ice creams. Ice cream was enriched with candied fruit, hazelnuts and chopped almonds. As well as the fruit juices, ice cream was flavoured with coffee, chocolate, cinnamon *(scorzonera)*, jasmine and mint.

***

Bacchus, the god of wine, bringing grapes from the Indies, gave wine to the mortals, a real panacea which brought joy. At least, this is what the Greeks who, it is said, then introduced wine to Sicily believed. It is surely no coincidence that the most ancient Sicilian colony, Naxos, used the Silenus as money. This was a figure of the Dionysian court holding the Kantharos, the typical drinking vessel. We now know that wild grapevine was common in a large part of the temperate area which includes most of the Mediterranean basin and that Greek mythology is attributed something which, after all, is a common legacy.

The strong and dense Sicilian wine, appreciated from ancient times, has long been used in Italy and abroad to prepare weaker wines. Only recently, our wines, treated with expertise, are becoming common in ever-vaster areas and markets.

From the dry whites of the area of Alcamo, to the reds of the Southern tip of the island - the cerasuolo wine of Vittoria and the nero of Pachino - now we have a whole series of quality-approved wines like those from the slopes of Etna. To these, we can add the wines treated with raisins or strongly sweetened wines, typical of the volcano areas of Pantelleria (*passito* wine, *muscatel* wine) and Lipari (*malvasia* wine). Nor do Sicilian wines lack a famous exponent. In fact, in the 18th century, Giovanni Meli, a famous poet from Palermo, sung the praises of the qualities of every single wine and, at the same time, criticised the pretensions of those who, having bottled and labelled it, sold the wine as if it were nectar from France. This was vanity of fashion, snobbish xenomania which is found in the habit of accompanying desserts with dry sparkling wines *(brut* or *extra-brut)* or, after dinner, guzzling whisky or cognac instead of the mistreated sweet wines.

Now, however, there has been a change in habits. It may be the current crisis or a change in taste that has led the people to look at the notebooks of their ancestors, the secrets of the convents, containing recipes for sweet wines and liquors and, with a slight change in the dose of the syrup, liquors made with citrus fruits, verbena, orange-blossom, mint, coffee, the ratafia of mulberries, strawberries, blackberries, walnut, herb and spice compounds mixed in various ways known as *centerbe* or *amari* (bitter aperitifs) and, finally, the age-old *anisetta* (aniseed cordial).

***

To close this piece, here is a final consideration. Think of the Sicilian who travels to any part of the Mediterranean - from Greece to Spain, from Syria to Magreb. If he is a connoisseur of the cuisine of the island, he can only discover similarities or find dishes which are identical or similar, as well as fragrances, tastes and colours which make him feel at home. They bring him back to Sicily. And anyone who has passed through Sicily, as master or servant, has left behind something of their own culture and has taken something special away with them.

Elda Joly

Little rice balls with meat
Arancineddi di risu cu a carni

For the rice:
- 1 kg (2 lb) Arborio rice
- 2.5 l (80 fl oz) water
- 50 g (2 oz) butter
- 2 sachets saffron
- salt

For the filling:
- 1 carrot
- 1 white onion
- 1 celery stick
- 500 g (1 lb) minced beef
- 200 g (8 oz) fresh peas
- 1 dash white wine
- 1 tbsp tomato puree
- 1 l (32 fl oz) water
- olive oil

For the breadcrumb coating:
- 1 egg
- 1/2 l (16 fl oz) water
- white flour
- breadcrumbs

Bring the water to the boil, pour in the rice, and cook over a moderate heat. When cooked, remove from the heat and add the butter and saffron. Leave to stand for about 2 minutes. Spread the rice on a plate and leave it to cool down completely.

In a separate saucepan, brown the finely chopped carrot, celery, and onion in oil. Add the meat and peas and brown well, then pour in the white wine. Add the tomato puree and dilute with water. Correct the salt and cook for about 25 minutes. When cooked, add the meat mixture to the rice. Take a small amount of mixture and roll into little "orange" balls.

For the binding mixture, dissolve the flour in the water. add the egg and mix well. Dip the little "oranges" in this mixture before coating with breadcrumbs. Deep fry and serve piping hot.

Fried caciocavallo cheese with a vinegar and oregano dressing
Caciucavaddu all'argintera

- 500 g (1 lb) medium-matured caciocavallo cheese
- 1/2 dl (1.5 fl oz) olive oil
- 2 garlic cloves
- 1 dash vinegar
- oregano
- white flour

Heat the oil in the frying pan, add the garlic and fry until brown. Flour the cheese, and brown on both sides over a medium heat until a light crust forms. Remove the pan from the heat, add a dash of vinegar, put the pan back on the heat, and leave it to evaporate. Serve with a sprinkling of oregano.

* photo

"Hooded" caciocavallo cheese
Caciucavaddu 'ncappucciatu

- 500 g (1 lb) fresh caciocavallo cheese
- 1/2 dl (1.5 fl oz) olive oil
- 1/2 tsp dried, finely chopped herbs (garlic, chervil, chilli, parsley)
- 4 eggs
- 1 dl (3 fl oz) fresh cream
- white flour
- ground black pepper

Dust the caciocavallo cheese with the flour and put it in a pan with the oil and herbs. Brown well on both sides over a moderate heat. In a bowl, beat the eggs together with the fresh cream. Pour into the pan and, as soon as it starts to solidify, take a fork and lightly flatten it over the cheese so that it is completely covered. Season with pepper and serve immediately.

Grilled artichokes
Cacocciuli arrustuti

- 6 artichokes
- salt
- olive oil

Discard the spiky parts of the artichokes, open them up slightly and add a pinch of salt between the leaves. When the charcoal is well alight, position the artichokes with the stalks pointing upwards. Wait until the outer leaves are charred, then remove from the heat and, after having discarded the burnt leaves, serve immediately with a drizzle of oil.

Artichokes with anchovies
Cacocciuli a viddanedda

- 6 artichokes
- 2 garlic cloves
- 2 anchovy fillets
- 1 parsley sprig
- olive oil
- salt

Discard the hard outer leaves and the spiky points of the artichokes, and wash under running water. Leave to rest in a container with water and the juice of half a lemon for about 1 hour. After such time, fill them with the slices of garlic, chopped parsley, anchovies and oil. Arrange them upright in a saucepan filled with salted water and cook over a low heat for about 15 minutes. Serve the artichokes cold with a drizzle of olive oil.

Variation: for a different filling you can use raisins, pine nuts, boned and mashed anchovies, mixed with lightly toasted breadcrumbs, pepper, oil and a few drops of lemon juice.

Fried artichokes
Cacocciuli fritti

- 6 artichokes
- 200 g (8 oz) white flour
- 3 eggs
- vegetable oil
- salt
- breadcrumbs

Discard the hard outer leaves and spiky points of the artichokes. Cut them into quarters and soak in water and lemon juice for a few hours. Boil the artichokes in salted water and lemon for about 5 minutes. Drain, then put them into a container, dust with flour, dip in beaten egg and coat with breadcrumbs. Fry them, only a few at a time, in hot oil.

Follow the above method if the artichokes are cut into thick wedges. If you cut the artichokes into eight, you can fry them without boiling them first.

Another method is to prepare a light runny batter by dissolving the flour in a little water and the juice of half a lemon, mixing with a fork until it is well-blended and stringy.

Artichokes in batter
Cacocciuli a pastetta

- 4 artichokes
- 200 g (8 oz) flour
- 20 g (0.5 oz) yeast
- a pinch of sugar
- 1/4 l (8 fl oz) warm water
- 3 eggs
- 1/2 lemon
- salt and pepper
- vegetable oil

In a bowl, dissolve the yeast in the warm water. Add the flour and the egg and make a batter. Add a pinch of sugar and then leave to stand for about 20 minutes.
Cut the artichokes into quarters and blanch for about 3 minutes in water with a pinch of salt and the juice of half a lemon. Drain well, dry and dip in the batter. Fry in hot oil a few at a time.

Cardoons in batter
Carduni a pastetta

- 4 cardoons
- 200 g (8 oz) white flour
- 20 g (0.5 oz) yeast
- a pinch of sugar
- 1/4 l (8 fl oz) water
- 3 eggs
- salt and pepper
- vegetable oil
- juice of 1 lemon

Boil the cardoons in water with salt and the juice of one lemon over a moderate heat. When cooked, drain and dip in a batter prepared by dissolving the yeast in warm water, adding the flour, a pinch of sugar, the eggs and mixing well. Leave the mixture to rest for about 20 minutes. Remove the cardoons from the batter and deep fry one at a time.

Artichoke bake
Gattò di cacocciuli

- 10 artichokes
- 1/2 white onion and parsley
- 3 fresh eggs
- olive oil
- 50 g (2 oz) grated caciocavallo cheese
- 10 g (0.3 oz) raisins and pine nuts
- a pinch of nutmeg
- salt
- a sprinkle of white flour

Discard the hard outer leaves of the artichokes. Cut into quarters, removing, the inner spikes, and boil for about 10 minutes in water with lemon juice. When cooked, drain and then cut into little pieces. Aside, beat the eggs in a bowl and add the nutmeg, cheese, raisins and pine nuts.
Pour the oil into a frying pan and lightly brown the onion over a low heat. Dust the artichokes with flour, add, and brown on both sides.
Add all the other ingredients and cook in the same way you would an omelette.
Serve hot or cold with a pinch of salt.

* photo

Poached cauliflower
Vrocculi affucati

- 1 cauliflower
- 2 dl (6 fl oz) olive oil
- 10 pitted black olives
- 4 garlic cloves cut into four
- water
- salt and pepper

Clean the cauliflower and cut into florets. Put the florets into a saucepan with the pitted olives, garlic and a pinch of salt. Add the water, cover with the lid, and cook over a moderate heat for about 15 minutes. Serve with a drizzle of oil and pepper.

Cauliflower in batter
Vrocculi a pastetta

- 1 cauliflower
- 250 g (10 oz) flour
- 15 g (0.5 oz) yeast
- a pinch of sugar
- 1/4 l (8 fl oz) warm water
- 3 eggs
- salt and pepper
- vegetable oil

Dissolve the yeast in the warm water, add the flour and mix with a fork. Add the eggs and mix to form a smooth batter. Add just a pinch of sugar and leave to stand for about 20 minutes.

Clean the cauliflower and soak for about 15 minutes in a container filled with salted water, putting the flower head in first.

Boil the cauliflower cut into large stalks in salted water for about 2 min. When cooked, drain and dry well. Slice the stalks and dip in the batter one at a time. Deep fry a few at a time.

Mussel soup
Zuppa di cozzi

- 1 kg (2 lbs) cleaned mussels
- 300 g (12 oz) peeled tomatoes
- 4 garlic cloves
- 2 dl (6 fl oz) olive oil
- freshly, finely chopped parsley
- salt and pepper

Clean the mussels and discard the little cords. Put all the raw ingredients (tomatoes, garlic, parsley, oil and mussels) in a saucepan and cook over a moderate heat covered with the lid. When the mussels have all opened up, add the pepper and serve with a drizzle of oil, chopped parsley and slices of fried bread.

* photo

Peppered mussels
'Mpipata di cozzi

- 1 kg (2 lbs) mussels
- 1 small ladle of water
- pepper

Clean the mussels and discard the little cords. Put all the mussels into a large pan, add a small ladle of water and cover with the lid. When all the mussels have opened up, serve with lots of pepper and lemon wedges.

"Rabbit-style" broad beans
Favi a cunigghiu

- 500 g (1 lb) broad beans
- 5 garlic cloves
- 1 l (32 fl oz) water
- olive oil
- oregano and salt

If the "black eyes" are quite big, remove them from the broad beans then boil the beans in water with salt and garlic for about 15 minutes. When cooked, drain but leave moist. Season with oregano and olive oil, and serve piping hot.

* photo

Boiled broad beans
Favi vugghiuti

- 500 g (1 lb) broad beans
- 1 sprig of wild fennel
- salt and pepper
- olive oil

If the "black eyes" are quite big, remove them from the broad beans then boil the beans in water with salt and wild fennel leaves for about 15 minutes. When the pulp is soft, serve with a drizzle of oil and freshly ground pepper.

Chickpea pancakes
Panelli fritti

- 1 l (32 fl oz) water
- 350 g (14 oz) chickpea flour
- 1 sprig of finely chopped parsley
- vegetable oil for frying
- salt and pepper

Dissolve the chickpea flour in salted, warm water stirring lightly so that no lumps form. Put the saucepan over the heat, add the parsley and the pepper and then mix well until it starts to thicken. Using a wooden spoon, spread a small amount of the mixture out on a platter or plate creating a very thin layer. When the mixture has cooled down, remove and cut into small triangle shapes. Deep fry in hot vegetable oil.

Stewed broad beans, peas and artichokes
Frittedda di favi, piseddi e cacocciuli

- 5 artichokes
- 500 g (1 lb) fresh peas
- 800 g (32 oz) young green broad beans
- 1 bunch of shallots (or 1 white onion)
- water
- salt and pepper
- olive oil

Clean the artichokes and remove both the hard leaves and spiky points. Cut them into little pieces and soak in water and lemon for about 15 minutes. In the meantime, shell the peas and beans. In a saucepan, brown the coarsely chopped onion in the oil. Add the artichokes, peas, beans, salt, pepper, and half a glass of water. Cook over a moderate heat for about 30 minutes, stirring every now and then with a wooden spoon. If necessary, add more water. Serve hot with a drizzle of oil.

Variation: when cooked, add a tablespoonful of sugar dissolved in half a glass of vinegar. Leave to rest for a few hours and serve cold.

Suggestion: mix short pasta cooked "al dente" to the variation.

Orange and herring salad

*'Nsalata d'aranci
e arenga ovata*

- 6 peeled navel oranges
- 2 spring onions (shallots)
- 150 g (6 oz) pitted green olives
- 100 g (4 oz) silver herrings
- water
- salt
- olive oil

Peel the oranges, remove the pith and cut into little pieces. Put them into a large bowl, crushing them slightly with a fork so that the juice flavours the salad. Cut the onions into thin slices, the olives into rings, and the herrings into pieces, mix with the oranges and add salt, oil and water.

Seafood salad
'Nsalata di mari

- 150 g (6 oz) squid rings
- 100 g (4 oz) peeled white shrimps
- 200 g (8 oz) small size octopus, cut into little pieces
- 400 g (16 oz) cleaned mussels
- olive oil
- parsley, finely chopped
- juice of 3 lemons
- salt and pepper

Boil the molluscs (squid and octopus) and the crustaceans (shrimps) separately in plenty of salted water. Aside, open the mussels. Put everything onto the serving dish and, when cold, add the olive oil, lemon juice, finely chopped parsley and pepper. Marinate for a couple of hours before serving.

Octopus salad
'Nsalata di purpu

- 1 small size octopus weighing approx. 1 kg (2 lbs)
- olive oil
- parsley, finely chopped
- salt and pepper
- juice of 1 lemon

Clean the octopus making sure that you rub the tentacles energetically with salt to remove the stickiness and the impurities from the suckers. Before boiling the octopus, plunge it three times into boiling salted water holding it by the head to make the tentacles curl up. Cook for about 20 minutes. Cut into little pieces. Season with pepper, oil and chopped parsley.

* photo

Snails with parsley and garlic
Babbaluci d'u Fistinu

- 1 kg (2 lbs) snails
- 4 garlic cloves
- 1 sprig of parsley, finely chopped

- 200 g (8 oz) breadcrumbs
- olive oil

Wash the snails and place them in a container with the breadcrumbs for 24 hours. Wash them thoroughly under running water, then boil in salted water for about 15 minutes initially over a very low heat and then gradually increasing the heat. Drain the snails and put then into a saucepan with oil, pepper, and the chopped parsley and garlic, quickly toss over a high heat. Leave to cool and give them a stir every now and then so that they soak up the flavour.

Variation: you may add a little tomato sauce.

Breaded aubergines
Milinciani a cutuletta

- 3 Tunisian aubergines (the variety with a round shape and a lighter colour)
- 4 fresh eggs
- breadcrumbs
- olive oil
- a pinch of salt
- white flour

Cut the aubergines into 1 cm (0.5 inch) thick slices, then wash and dry them. Beat the eggs together with the salt in a bowl.

Dust the slices with flour, dip in the beaten egg, coat with breadcrumbs and deep fry in olive oil. When cooked, dry off the excessive oil on kitchen paper before serving.

* photo

"Canazzo" aubergines
Milinciani a canazzu

- 4 aubergines
- 200 g (8 oz) peeled tomatoes
- 1 white onion
- water
- olive oil
- salt and pepper

Coarsely dice the aubergines and soak in a container with water and salt for about 15 minutes. Rinse under running water and drain thoroughly. Put the oil, the sliced onion, the aubergines, the chopped peeled tomatoes, a pinch of salt and finally the pepper into a saucepan. Cook over a moderate heat with half a glass of water for about 15 minutes. Cool before serving.

Variation: you may add coarsely chopped peppers and potatoes to the aubergines.

Aubergine *"caponata"*
'Capunata di milinciani

- 4 medium size aubergines
- 1 white onion, diced
- 2 celery stalks
- 70 g (3 oz) pitted green olives
- 40 g (2 oz) Pantelleria capers
- 1 dl (3 fl oz) white vinegar
- 1 tbsp sugar
- 1 tbsp tomato puree
- salt
- olive oil

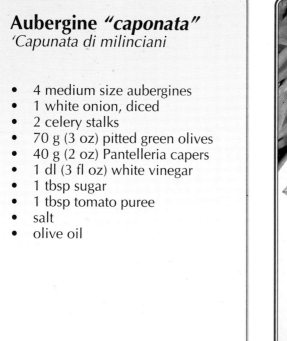

Coarsely dice the aubergines, sprinkle them with salt and leave them to rest in a colander so that they deposit the bitter liquid. In a saucepan, boil the chopped celery, green olives and desalted capers for about 10 minutes. When cooked, drain and set aside, reserving the water that can be used to correct the density of the mixture. Fry the aubergines and set aside. Brown the onion in the oil for about 2 minutes and then add the prepared vegetable mixture and brown for a further 5 minutes. Add the vinegar and cook until it evaporates. Then add the sugar and the tomato puree and mix thoroughly, adding the vegetable cooking water. Correct the salt and cook for a further 10 minutes, adding the diced aubergines towards the end. Serve the *caponata* cold.

Fried aubergines
Milinciani a quagghia

- 4 medium size aubergines
- vegetable oil
- salt and pepper

Cut each aubergine into 6 wedges without cutting through the stalk, and soak them in salted water for about 25 minutes. Wash and pat dry with kitchen paper. Deep fry one at a time in a little saucepan filled with oil. Add pepper, salt, and serve piping hot.

Dressed grilled aubergines
Milinciani 'rrustuti cu a menta e l'agghia

- 4 local aubergines
- 3 garlic cloves, cut into quarters
- a dash of vinegar
- fresh mint leaves
- olive oil
- salt and pepper

Slice the aubergines and soak in a container with salted water for about 15 minutes. Drain and pat dry. Place the slices on a hot grill and cook on both sides. When cooked, season with oil, garlic, pepper, a dash of vinegar and plenty of fresh mint.

*photo

Aubergine roulades
Milinciani chini ammugghiati

- 2 local aubergines, cut into slices
- 200 g (8 oz) fresh tomato sauce
- vegetable oil
- salt

For the filling:
- 50 g (2 oz) fresh caciocavallo cheese, chopped
- 50 g (2 oz) ham, chopped
- 50 g (2 oz) salami, chopped
- 50 g (2 oz) mortadella, chopped
- 10 slices of sandwich loaf bread, crumbled
- 2 eggs

Soak the aubergine slices in salted water for about 15 minutes, then wash and pat dry. Deep fry in vegetable oil. Mix all the ingredients for the filling in a bowl. Shape this mixture into little oval balls, place on the fried aubergine slices, roll and arrange them in a baking tin. With a spoon, cover the rolls with tomato sauce and bake in the oven.

Aubergine *"parmigiana"*
Milinciani a parmiciana

- 2 aubergines, sliced
- 300 g (12 oz) fresh tomato sauce
- 150 g (6 oz) grated parmesan cheese
- fresh basil
- vegetable oil

Soak the aubergines, after having cut them lengthways, in salt and water for about 30 minutes.
Wash, dry and then fry them for two minutes in hot oil.
Put them in the serving dish in layers alternated with the tomato sauce and parmesan cheese. Garnish with fresh basil.

*photo

Stuffed aubergines
Milincianeddi 'mbuttunati

- 12 local small size aubergines
- 6 garlic cloves, cut into quarters
- 200 g (8 oz) fresh caciocavallo cheese
- fresh tomato sauce
- vegetable oil for frying
- fresh mint
- salt and pepper

Soak the aubergines in a container with salt and water for about 1 hour, after having made little holes in the skin with a sharp knife, and then wash and dry them. Stuff the little holes with garlic, cheese, mint, salt and pepper. Fry them in hot oil for one minute. Add them to the sauce and cook for a further 10 minutes.

Variation: add a tablespoon of sugar dissolved in half a glass of vinegar to the tomato sauce.

Aubergines in oil
Milinciani sott'ogghiu

- 8 small aubergines, cut into wedges
- 1 l (32 fl oz) water
- 1/2 l (16 fl oz) vinegar
- salt
- olive oil

Peel the aubergines and cut them into wedges. Boil for about 15 minutes in water, vinegar and salt. Drain them and when the are completely dry, put them into a glass jar and cover with oil.
If desired, oregano, a few cloves of garlic (whole or chopped), and some pieces of chilli may be added.

Dressed olives
Alivi cunzati

- 200 g (8 oz) green olives
- 2 tbsp extra virgin oil
- a dash of vinegar
- 2 garlic cloves
- fresh mint

Crush the olives and season with the sliced garlic, mint leaves, a dash of vinegar and the extra virgin oil. Prepare 3 hours before serving.

There are many different ways of dressing the olives, which depend on family traditions. They can be served with pickled vegetables, or they can be prepared using basil in place of the garlic, or oregano in place of the mint leaves. Another popular way of preparing olives in Sicily is to pickle them in brine (1l (32 fl oz) water and 150 g (6 oz) of salt) and to preserve them in a large jar as in the following recipe.

* photo

Crushed olives
Alivi scacciati

- 1 kg (2 lbs) green olives
- 1 l (32 fl oz) water
- 150 g (6 oz) salt
- 3 garlic cloves
- 1/2 tbsp oregano

Using a wooden spoon, crush the green olives and put them into water (without salt) for 3 days, changing the water every day.

Afterwards, add water, salt, oregano, garlic and, if you like, also a few salted anchovy fillets.

Oven baked potatoes

- 1 kg (2 lbs) potatoes
- olive oil
- salt and rosemary
- black pepper

Peel the potatoes and cut them into wedges. Put them into a baking tin with oil, salt, pepper and rosemary. Give them a quick stir, then bake in pre-heated 180°C (350°F) oven for about 20 minutes.
If desired, a medium size, finely sliced onion can be added.

Fried potato croquettes
Cazzilli

- 1 kg (2 lbs) potatoes
- 1 sprig of parsley, chopped
- 1 tsp fennel seeds
- vegetable oil
- salt and pepper
- 3 eggs

Boil the potatoes in salted water, peel, mash and then pass through a vegetable mill. Put the potato purée into a bowl and add salt, pepper, chopped parsley and fennel seeds. Then mix in the egg yolks, one at a time. Grease the palm of one hand with a little oil and shape the croquettes into little cylinders. Deep fry the croquettes in hot oil.

Pepper ragout
Pipi a tuttu dintra

- 4 peppers
- 2 onions
- 300 g (12 oz) peeled tomatoes
- 1/2 dl (1 fl oz) white wine
- salt and pepper
- olive oil

Coarsely chop the peppers and discard the seeds. In a saucepan, sauté the onion in olive oil. Add the peppers and cook over a low heat. Add a dash of white wine. Mix in the squashed peeled tomatoes, salt and pepper. Cook over a moderate heat for a further 15 minutes.

* photo

Roast peppers
Pipi arrustuti

- 4 red and yellow peppers
- 3 garlic cloves, cut into quarters
- a dash of vinegar
- basil
- olive oil
- a pinch of salt

Place the peppers on the grill and cook over a moderate heat on both sides. When cooked, leave to cool, and then peel. Arrange the peppers on a plate and season with oil, garlic, vinegar, basil and salt. Prepare at least 3 hours before serving.

Peppers can also be baked in the oven and seasoned with the juice of one lemon instead of vinegar.

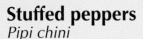

Stuffed peppers
Pipi chini

- 4 peppers
- 1 white onion
- 300 g (12 oz) breadcrumbs
- 150 g (6 oz) fresh caciocavallo cheese
- 1 dl (3 fl oz) olive oil
- 100 g (4 oz) peeled tomatoes
- 2 garlic cloves, chopped
- salt
- water

In a frying pan, toast the breadcrumbs in oil and garlic. In a bowl, mix the toasted breadcrumbs with the diced caciocavallo cheese, the squashed peeled tomatoes, the olive oil and salt and set aside.

In the meantime, cut the peppers in half, remove the seeds and then blanch them. Stuff with the breadcrumb mixture and bake in the oven for about 10 minutes, remembering to pour a little olive oil or half a glass of water into the baking dish. Add a drizzle of oil and serve.

Stuffed tomatoes
Pummarori a viddana

- 8 firm, ripe tomatoes
- 1 dl (3 fl oz) olive oil
- a sprig of basil
- a sprig of parsley
- a sprig of mint
- salt and pepper
- 4 garlic cloves

Cut the tomatoes in half, remove the seeds and leave them upside down to drain.
Finely chop the fresh herbs and garlic and season with salt and pepper.
Arrange the tomatoes in a greased baking tin and stuff with the chopped herb mixture. Drizzle a little oil over them and bake in a pre-heated oven for about 20 minutes. Serve hot.

Variation: fill the tomatoes with bread-crumbs, diced caciocavallo cheese and diced salami.

Flat-fried sardines
Sardi a linguati

- 500 g (1 lb) fresh sardines
- sufficient vinegar to cover the sardines
- white flour
- olive oil

Remove the scales and open up the sardines, starting from the head and working downwards, but leaving the tail attached to the fish. Using your thumb work upwards so that they are well descaled. Put the sardines in a bowl and marinate in vinegar for about 30 minutes. Drain, dust with flour and fry in hot oil.

* photo

Genoese courgettes in sweet and sour sauce
Cucuzzeddi agro e duci

- 4 Genoese courgettes
- 4 garlic cloves, cut into quarters
- olive oil for dressing
- a dash of vinegar
- a sprinkle of sugar
- salt
- plenty of fresh mint leaves
- vegetable oil for frying

After having removed alternated strips of the green outer skin, cut the courgettes into approximately 1 cm thick slices then deep fry in vegetable oil. In a frying pan, brown the garlic in the olive oil. Add the sugar, making sure it dissolves, and finally a dash of vinegar. Pour the sauce over the courgettes, leave to cool and serve with plenty of fresh mint.

Sicilian-style stuffed courgettes
Cucuzzeddi a gratè

- 4 Genoese courgettes
- 1 white onion
- 300 g (12 oz) breadcrumbs
- 150 g (6 oz) fresh caciocavallo cheese
- 100 g (4 oz) peeled tomatoes
- 1 dl (3 fl oz) olive oil
- salt and pepper

Cut the courgettes in half lengthways and scoop out the pulp. Blanch in salted water for about 5 minutes; drain, and dry. In a frying pan, brown the minced onion, add the breadcrumbs and toast for about 5 minutes. In a bowl, mix the breadcrumb mixture with the diced caciocavallo cheese, the peeled tomatoes and the olive oil. Correct the salt and add a little pepper. Grease a baking tin with oil and arrange the courgettes after having stuffed them with the filling. Bake in a pre-heated oven for about 15 minutes.

Sweet and sour pumpkin
Cucuzza russa agro e duci

- 400 g (16 oz) pumpkin
- 4 garlic cloves
- 2 dl (6 fl oz) olive oil
- a dash of vinegar
- fresh mint leaves
- vegetable oil for frying
- salt
- a sprinkle of sugar

After having removed the skin, cut the pumpkin into slices of about 1 cm (0.5 inch) each, then deep fry in vegetable oil over a moderate heat. In a separate frying pan, brown the garlic in the olive oil, add the sugar and then the vinegar. Cook until the vinegar evaporates. Arrange the pumpkin on the serving dish and pour over the sauce. Cover with fresh mint leaves and serve cold.

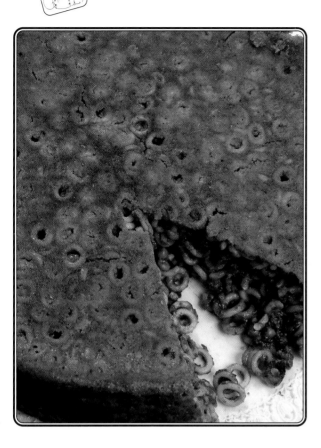

Anelletti pasta with minced meat
Anelletti cu a carne capuliata

- 400 g (16 oz) anelletti pasta (rings)
- 1 onion
- 300 g (12 oz) tomato puree
- 300 g (12 oz) beef, coarsely minced
- 300 g (12 oz) pork, coarsely minced
- 200 g (8 oz) peas
- 250 g (10 oz) Neapolitan-style salami
- 250 g (10 oz) fresh primosale cheese (or pecorino)
- 250 g (10 oz) fresh caciocavallo cheese
- 1 dl (3 fl oz) dry white wine
- 2 tsp fennel seeds
- 2 dl (6 fl oz) olive oil
- salt and pepper
- water

Sauté the chopped onion in the oil, add the beef and pork meat, and crumble the meat using a wooden spoon. Pour in the wine and cook till it evaporates. Add the tomato puree and dilute with enough water to make a runny sauce, add the fennel seeds and cook over a moderate heat for about 30 minutes. In another saucepan blanch the peas in salted water and dice the salami and cheese. As soon as the meat is cooked, add the salami and peas. Boil the pasta in plenty of salted water for about 20 minutes. Drain and then pour into the saucepan with the sauce. Add the diced cheese, mix quickly and serve hot or warm.

Variation: put the pasta and sauce mixture into a greased baking tin coated with breadcrumbs. Drizzle with oil and cover the top with breadcrumbs. Bake in a hot oven for about 30 minutes. Leave to cool, turn out and serve warm.

Sicilian-style stuffed cannelloni

* 12 sheets of cannelloni (fresh pasta)

For the filling:
* 1 carrot
* 1 onion
* 2 celery stalks
* 2 dl (7 fl oz) olive oil
* 400 g (1 lb) minced beef
* 150 g (6 oz) peas
* 1 dl (3.5 fl oz) white wine
* 200 g (8 oz) tomato puree
* salt and pepper
* water

For the béchamel sauce:
* 1 l (32 fl oz) milk
* 200 g (8 oz) butter
* 100 g (4 oz) white flour
* salt and nutmeg

In a pot, boil the pasta sheets in salted water; drain, then pass them through cold, salted water. In a saucepan, boil three quarters of the milk with the salt, nutmeg and butter; dissolve the flour in the left over milk. When the milk boils, mix in the milk and flour, stirring carefully until it thickens.

In another saucepan, sauté the chopped carrot, onion and celery in the oil, add the minced beef and peas; brown well, and add a few dashes of wine. Add the tomato puree, dilute with enough water to make a rather thick sauce. Add salt, pepper, and cook for about 20 minutes over a moderate heat.

After having drained the pasta sheets thoroughly lay them out on the table. Put some filling onto each pasta sheet horizontally then roll up the pasta to form the cannelloni. Grease a rectangular baking dish with butter, cover it with a layer of béchamel sauce and add the cannelloni. Cover with the remaining béchamel, a few knobs of butter and a handful of grated Parmesan cheese. Bake in a pre-heated 150°C (300°F) oven and serve piping hot.

Pasta and cauliflower soup
Pasta cu i vrocculi

- 300 g (12 oz) margherita pasta, broken up into little pieces
- 600 g (24 oz) small cauliflower florets
- 4 garlic cloves, sliced
- water
- 2 dl (6 fl oz) olive oil
- salt and pepper

Clean the cauliflower, cut it up into pieces and soak for a few minutes. Boil in plenty of salted water. When almost cooked, add the pasta and cook for just over 10 minutes. Finally add the garlic, browned in oil, correct the salt, add a little pepper and serve hot.

Sicilian broccoli and pasta soup
Pasta cu i sparaceddi

- 300 g (12 oz) margherita pasta, broken up into little pieces
- 2 bunches of broccoli
- 4 garlic cloves
- water
- olive oil
- salt and pepper

Clean the broccoli, discarding the hard outer leaves, wash and then dice them in approximately 1 cm (0.5 inch) pieces. Soak for about 30 minutes, drain, then boil in plenty of salted water for about 10 minutes. In a separate saucepan, brown the garlic in the oil and pour it over the broccoli, after having first adjusted the amount of water. Add the pasta and cook for just over ten minutes. Correct the salt, add pepper and serve with the cooking water.

Pasta and cabbage soup
Pasta cu i cavuli

- 300 g (12 oz) margherita pasta, broken into little pieces
- 2 cabbages
- 4 garlic cloves, sliced
- water
- 2 dl (6 fl oz) olive oil
- salt and pepper

Wash, then soak the cabbage leaves after first having cut them into approximately 1 cm strips, along with the peeled and diced stalk. Drain and put into a pot with boiling salted water. When almost cooked, add the pasta and continue cooking. Adjust the amount of water, correct the salt and serve with pepper.

Variation: add garlic browned in oil to the cabbage, but, in this case the amount of water needs adjusting before adding the pasta.

Pasta and bean soup
Pasta cu i fasola

- 300 g (12 oz) margherita pasta, broken up into little pieces
- 500 g (1 lb) dried beans
- 200 g (8 oz) bacon fat
- 150 g (6 oz) peeled tomatoes
- 1 onion
- 1 celery stalk
- water
- salt and pepper

Soak the beans in a pot. After about 12 hours, add the diced tomatoes, the onion, and celery and cook for about 15 minutes over a moderate heat. Slightly brown the bacon fat in a frying pan and add to the beans; adjust the water, add salt, pepper and then the pasta. Cook for a further 10 minutes over a moderate heat then serve piping hot.

Variations: it is possible to do without the bacon fat by adding a drizzle of oil before serving. Fresh beans can also be used, following the same procedure.

Pasta and broad bean soup
Pasta cu i favuzzi frischi

- 300 g (12 oz) Jolanda pasta
- 600 g (24 oz) fresh broad beans
- 1 onion, sliced
- water
- 2 dl (6 fl oz) olive oil
- salt and pepper

Shell the beans, leaving them whole if small and tender. In a saucepan, brown the onion in the oil, pour in the beans and enough water to cover. Add salt, pepper, and cook for about 10 minutes. Add the pasta and cook for a further 8 minutes. Serve hot.

Variation: the beans can be served with fried croutons instead of pasta.

Pasta and lentil soup
Pasta cu i linticchia

- 300 g (12 oz) small ditalini pasta
- 500 g (1 lb) dried lentils
- 150 g (6 oz) peeled tomatoes
- 1 bunch of wild fennel
- 1 onion
- 1 carrot (optional)
- 1 celery stalk (optional)
- water
- salt and pepper
- olive oil

Put the lentils into a pot, cover with water and soak for about 12 hours.
Add the sliced onion, the chopped fennel leaves and, if desired, the celery, carrot and tomatoes; cook over a moderate heat for about 15 minutes. Add the pasta, correct the salt, add a little pepper and cook for a further 10 minutes. Serve with a drizzle of oil.

Variation: serve the lentil soup with fried croutons instead of pasta.

Pasta and courgette leaf soup
Pasta cu i tinnirumi

- 300 g (12 oz) margherita pasta, broken up into little pieces
- 2 bunches of courgette leaves, cleaned and cut into pieces
- 4 garlic cloves, sliced
- 150 g (6 oz) peeled tomatoes
- 1 dl (3 fl oz) olive oil
- salt and pepper
- 150 g (6 oz) medium-matured caciocavallo cheese
- a sprig of basil (optional)

Clean, cut into pieces and then boil the courgette leaves in boiling salted water. Cook for about 10 minutes, then add the pasta. In a little saucepan, lightly brown the garlic in the oil and add the chopped tomatoes after having removed all the seeds, (and if desired, the basil). Cook for just a few minutes. Pour off any excess water from the pasta and add the sauce. Correct the salt, add pepper and, before removing from the heat, sprinkle with the diced cheese.

Pasta and courgette soup
Pasta cu a cucuzza

- 300 g (12 oz) spaghetti, broken up into little pieces
- 1 long courgette
- 150 g (6 oz) peeled tomatoes
- 1 large onion
- 150 g (6 oz) mature caciocavallo cheese
- water
- olive oil
- salt and pepper
- a sprig of fresh basil

Peel and dice the courgette. In a saucepan, brown the onion in oil and add the courgette. Add the tomatoes, water, salt and pepper and cook for about 18 minutes over a moderate heat. Adjust the amount of water, add the pasta. When cooked, add the diced cheese and cover with basil leaves. Serve hot.

Pasta with red anchovies
Pasta c'anciova russa e a muddica

- 400 g (16 oz) margherita or reginella pasta
- 40 g (2 oz) anchovy paste
- 200 g (8 oz) tomato puree
- 2 garlic cloves, sliced
- water
- toasted breadcrumbs
- olive oil
- salt and pepper

In a frying pan, brown the sliced garlic in the olive oil. Add the anchovy paste making sure that it dissolves. Mix in the tomato puree and blend thoroughly. Dilute the sauce with the water, correct the salt, add pepper and cook over a moderate heat for about 10 minutes. Drain the pasta, add the sauce and serve topped with toasted breadcrumbs.

Variation: raisins and pine nuts may be added to the anchovy paste to give the sauce a sweeter taste.

Spaghetti with tuna roe
Pasta cu l'ovu di tunnu

- 400 g (16 oz) spaghetti
- 200 g (8 oz) minced tuna roe
- 4 garlic cloves, sliced
- 1 sprig of parsley, finely chopped
- 2 dl (6 fl oz) olive oil
- salt and pepper
- 1 ladle of the pasta cooking water

Cook the pasta in plenty of salted water. In a saucepan, brown the garlic in the oil, add the tuna roe, a ladle of the pasta cooking water and mix gently with a wooden spoon.
Add chopped parsley. Drain the pasta, leaving it slightly moist. Pour over the sauce and serve with pepper and, if desired, top with more ground tuna roe.

Spaghetti with a piquant sauce
Pasta a carrittera

- 400 g (16 oz) spaghetti
- 3 garlic cloves
- 4 tbsp olive oil
- 1 sprig of parsley, finely chopped
- salt and pepper or ground chilli

In a bowl, soak the minced garlic and the chopped parsley in the oil.
Cook the pasta in plenty of salted water and drain, leaving it slightly moist. Mix with the dressing, add pepper and serve hot.

Variation: brown the garlic in the oil, add the chopped parsley and, if desired, anchovy paste dissolved in a little water. Add pepper and sprinkle with toasted breadcrumbs.

* photo

Pasta with cauliflower
Pasta cu i vrocculi arriminati

- 400 g (16 oz) bucato pasta
- 1 cauliflower cut into florets
- 4 anchovy fillets
- 50 g (2 oz) tomato puree
- 100 g (4 oz) raisins and pine nuts
- 1 chopped onion
- the cauliflower cooking water
- 2 dl (6 fl oz) olive oil
- salt and pepper

Wash and cut the cauliflower into florets, then boil in a pot. Using a strainer, drain and reserve the cooking water. In a saucepan, brown the onion and the anchovy fillets in the oil. Add the raisins, pine nuts, tomato puree and the boiled cauliflower. Pour in a few ladles of the cauliflower cooking water and cook, mashing the cauliflower with a wooden spoon until creamy. Correct the salt and add pepper. Cook the pasta for about 8 minutes in the cauliflower cooking water. Drain, and mix with the cauliflower sauce. Leave to rest for a while and serve warm.

Variation: use powdered saffron in place of the tomato puree.

Spaghetti with mussels

- 400 g (16 oz) spaghetti
- 1 kg (2 lbs) fresh mussels
- 2 anchovy fillets in oil
- 4 garlic cloves, sliced
- 1 sprig of parsley, finely chopped
- 2 dl (6 fl oz) olive oil
- salt and pepper
- water

Clean the mussels, and discard the little cords. Put them into a pan, add a ladle of water, then cover and cook over a moderate heat for about 5 minutes.
In a frying pan, brown the garlic in the oil, then add the anchovy fillets and let them dissolve. Add the shelled mussels, the pepper and the finely chopped parsley. Dilute with the mussels' cooking water and cook over a moderate heat for about 3 minutes.
Cook the spaghetti "al dente" in plenty of boiling salted water, drain, then mix with the mussel sauce.

Pasta with dried broad beans
Pasta cu u macco

- 200 g (8 oz) margherita pasta, broken up into little pieces
- 600 g (24 oz) dried broad beans
- 1 bunch of wild fennel, finely chopped
- 1 onion, finely chopped
- water
- 2 dl (6 fl oz) olive oil
- salt and pepper

Soak the broad beans into a pot, preferably earthenware, for at least 12 hours. Then mix with the onion and fennel leaves and cook over a moderate heat until they become thick and creamy. Cook the pasta separately, drain, and mix with the sauce. Correct the salt, add pepper and serve with a drizzle of oil.

Variation: add a diced tomato. Use fried croutons instead of the pasta.

Fried pasta
Pasta fritta

- 400 g (16 oz) spaghetti
- 300 g (12 oz) fresh tomato sauce
- 2 dl (6 fl oz) olive oil

The characteristic of this dish comes from the fact that the spaghetti is cooked beforehand, mixed with the tomato sauce, cooled and then fried in oil. The secret is letting the spaghetti form a crust whilst it is being fried. It is also a good way of "recycling" left over pasta.

* photo

Pasta with prawns
Pasta cu i 'ammari

- 400 g (16 oz) spaghetti
- 20 medium size prawns
- 200 g (8 oz) peeled tomatoes
- a dash of white wine
- 4 garlic cloves
- 1 sprig of parsley, finely chopped
- 2 dl (6 fl oz) olive oil
- salt and pepper

Shell the prawns, being careful not to remove the head. In a frying pan, brown the garlic with the prawns in the oil. Add a few dashes of white wine, then the peeled tomatoes. Correct the salt and moisten with a ladle of hot water. Cook for about 5 minutes over a moderate heat. Boil the spaghetti separately until "al dente", mix with the prawn sauce, pour onto the serving dish and sprinkle with parsley and pepper. Arrange the prawns on top and serve hot.

Variation: instead of the prawns you can use two lobsters cut in half, having first gutted them and removed the sack from behind the head. Cook in the same way as for the prawns.

Cuttlefish ink pasta
Pasta cu u nivuru d'i sicci

- 400 g (16 oz) linguine pasta
- 2 cuttlefish weighing about 300 g (12 oz) each
- 4 garlic cloves, finely chopped
- a dash of white wine
- 200 g (8 oz) tomato puree
- water
- 2 dl (6 fl oz) olive oil
- salt and pepper
- salted ricotta cheese (optional)

Clean the cuttlefish, remove the small black ink sacks putting them into a bowl. Squash the sacks, and dilute with a little water. Cut the cuttlefish into strips and sauté in a saucepan with garlic and oil When brown, add a dash of wine, the tomato puree and the ink. Add more water, correct the salt, add pepper and then cook for about 15 minutes over a moderate heat. Boil the pasta in plenty of salted water. When cooked "al dente", drain and mix with the sauce over the heat for a few more minutes. Serve hot.

Variation: sprinkle finely grated salted ricotta cheese over the pasta.

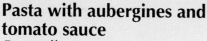

Pasta with aubergines and tomato sauce
Pasta alla Norma

- 400 g (16 oz) penne pasta
- 2-3 dl (6-9 fl oz) tomato sauce
- 1 medium size aubergine, diced
- 50 g (2 oz) grated baked ricotta cheese
- salt and pepper
- fresh basil
- vegetable oil

In a frying pan, deep fry the diced aubergine.
Cook the pasta in salted water and drain when "al dente". Pour back into the pot, sprinkle with the grated ricotta cheese and mix quickly. Add the tomato sauce, aubergines, pepper and mix once again.
When serving the pasta, garnish with fresh basil leaves.

Pasta with swordfish and mint
Pasta cu pisci spata e amenta frisca

- 400 g (16 oz) bavette pasta
- 600 g (24 oz) swordfish, diced
- 300 g (12 oz) peeled tomatoes
- 1 dl (3 fl oz) white wine
- 4 garlic cloves
- lots of fresh mint
- 2 dl (6 fl oz) olive oil
- salt and pepper

In a saucepan, brown the garlic in the oil, add the diced swordfish and sauté. Add a few dashes of wine and the peeled tomatoes. Correct the salt, add pepper and the fresh mint. In the meantime, cook the pasta until "al dente", drain, mix with the swordfish sauce and serve hot.

Pasta with Sicilian-style *"pesto"*

- 400 g (16 oz) spaghetti
- 2 sprigs of mint
- 2 sprigs of basil
- 50 g (2 oz) almonds
- 2 garlic cloves
- 30 g (1 oz) grated caciocavallo cheese
- 1 dl (3 fl oz) olive oil
- salt and pepper

Finely chop the basil, the mint, the garlic and the almonds. Add the oil, the caciocavallo cheese, salt and pepper. Leave to rest for a couple of hours. Boil the spaghetti in plenty of salted water, drain and mix with the sauce. Serve piping hot.

Pasta with peas
Pasta cu i pisedduzzi frischi

- 400 g (16 oz) ditali pasta
- 500 g (1 lb) shelled peas
- 2 dl (6 fl oz) olive oil
- 1 onion, sliced
- 1 sachet of saffron (optional)
- water
- salt and pepper
- grated parmesan or pecorino cheese

In a small pan, sauté the chopped onion in the oil. Add a ladle of water, salt, pepper and the peas, and cook for about 15 minutes. If you want to give the dish a little colour, add the saffron and remove from the heat. Boil the pasta, drain, add to the peas and serve with grated cheese.

*photo

Pasta with peeled tomatoes
Pasta cu pummarori a picchiu pacchiu

- 400 g (16 oz) trenette pasta
- 500 g (1 lb) ripe tomatoes
- 4 garlic cloves, sliced

- 1 sprig of basil
- olive oil
- salt and pepper

Blanch the tomatoes in hot water for about 2 minutes.
Peel, cut them in half and remove the seeds. Dice and then sauté in the oil with the garlic. Add salt and pepper. Cook over a medium heat for about 5 minutes. Finally, add the basil leaves. Cook the pasta in salted water, drain and add the sauce. Stir well before serving.

Pasta with pork meat sauce
Pasta cu u porcu a ragù

- 400 g (16 oz) bucatini pasta
- 400 g (16 oz) minced pork
- 1 onion
- 1 carrot
- 2 celery stalks
- a dash of dry white wine
- 150 g (6 oz) tomato puree
- fennel seeds
- water
- 2 dl (6 fl oz) olive oil
- salt and pepper
- 400 g (16 oz) fresh ricotta cheese (optional)

In a saucepan, sauté the chopped onion, celery and carrot, then add the minced meat. Add a dash of wine and cook whilst gently breaking up the meat into little pieces. Mix in the tomato puree and the fennel seeds. Add as much water as is necessary to make a runny sauce; cover and cook for at least 20 minutes over a moderate heat, stirring from time to time. Correct the salt and add pepper.
Boil the pasta in plenty of salted water. When "al dente" drain, mix with the meat sauce and serve piping hot.

Variation: after having mixed the pasta with the meat sauce, top with crumbled ricotta cheese.
As this dish is rather popular in the area of Agrigento, it is also called "Agrigento-style pasta".

Pasta with sea-urchins
Pasta cu li rizza

- 400 g (16 oz) spaghetti
- 60 large sea-urchins
- 4 garlic cloves, sliced
- 1 sprig of parsley, finely chopped
- 2 dl (6 fl oz) olive oil
- a dash of dry white wine
- salt and pepper
- a ladle of the pasta cooking water

Cook the pasta and in the meantime, in a frying pan, brown the garlic slices in oil, then add a dash of white wine. Add parsley, pepper, a ladle of the pasta cooking water. Drain the pasta "al dente", leaving it just a little moist. Then mix with the sauce and top with the sea-urchin corals. Serve piping hot.

Pasta with fresh ricotta cheese
Pasta c'a ricotta frisca

- 400 g (16 oz) margherita or reginella pasta
- 200 g (8 oz) fresh ricotta cheese
- 2 ladles of the pasta cooking water
- salt and black pepper or chilli
- grated parmesan or pecorino cheese

Cook the pasta in salted water. Drain and put back in the pot. In a bowl, using a fork, mix the fresh ricotta cheese with the hot pasta water. Pour over the pasta, mix and serve with lots of grated cheese (parmesan or pecorino) and ground black pepper.

Variation: Depending on personal taste, a few tablespoonfuls of fresh tomato sauce or peas cooked together with strips of ham may be added.

Pasta with sardines (and wild fennel)
Pasta cu i sardi

Even if pasta with sardines is a typical dish in Western Sicily, it can be prepared in many different ways. Not everybody follows the same recipe: there are people who put saffron into the boiling water before throwing in the pasta, those who add tomato puree, and others who prefer to add toasted breadcrumbs. Some use lots of sardines and some do not, some add a dash of white wine and others toasted almonds. The following recipe is the most popular one:

- 400g (16 oz) maccheroncelli pasta
- 1 small white onion, finely chopped
- 50 g (2 oz) olive oil
- 4 salted sardine fillets
- 50 g (2 oz) raisins and pine nuts
- 1 bunch of fresh fennel
- 400 g (16 oz) fresh, boned sardines
- salt and pepper
- 1 sachet of saffron

In a saucepan, brown the onion in the oil, add the fillets and let them dissolve. Then add the raisins and pine nuts and brown for a minute or so. Boil the fennel separately in plenty of salted water, drain and chop finely with a sharp, pointed knife, reserving the water. Add the fennel to the sauce, cover with the fennel cooking water and bring to the boil for about five minutes. Finally, add the fresh sardines, correct the salt, add pepper and cook for a further five minutes. Bring the fennel cooking water to a boil again and cook the pasta with the saffron. Drain and mix with the sauce. Garnish the dish with an open sardine. Serve warm.

Pasta with red tuna
Pasta c'a tunnina

- 400 g (16 oz) rigatoni pasta
- 300 g (12 oz) tuna, fresh or in oil
- 50 g (2 oz) tomato puree
- 2 garlic cloves
- water
- a dash of dry white wine
- 1 dl (3 fl oz) olive oil
- fresh mint
- salt and pepper

In a saucepan, brown the garlic in the oil, add the tuna (fresh or in oil) broken up into little pieces. Add a dash of white wine and finally the tomato puree. Dilute with water, correct the salt, add pepper and cook over a moderate heat for about 15 minutes. Cook the pasta in plenty of boiling salted water for about 12 minutes. Drain, mix with the sauce and serve with plenty of fresh mint leaves.

Variation: if you are using tuna in oil squeeze the juice of half a lemon over it, add some finely chopped parsley, desalted capers and garlic. Pour over the cooked pasta, stir thoroughly and serve.

Trapani-style pasta
Pasta a trapanisi

- 400 g (16 oz) bavette pasta
- 4 large, ripe tomatoes
- 4 garlic cloves
- 3 tbsp olive oil
- 1 sprig of fresh basil
- salt and pepper

Blanch the tomatoes in hot water for about 2 minutes.
Peel the tomatoes, cut them in half and remove the seeds. Coarsely chop the flesh of the tomatoes together with the garlic and basil. Correct the salt and add pepper. Mix with the olive oil, and marinate for a few hours. Cook the pasta in salted water and when "al dente", drain, mix with the sauce and serve.

Spaghetti with clams
Pasta cu l'arceddi

- 400 g (16 oz) spaghetti
- 1 kg (2 lbs) large clams
- 4 garlic cloves, sliced
- 1 sprig of parsley, finely chopped
- 2 dl (6 fl oz) olive oil
- a dash of dry white wine
- pepper

In a little saucepan, brown the sliced garlic in the oil, add the clams, and the wine, and when it evaporates, cover and cook until the clams have opened. Add the pepper and the chopped parsley. Boil the pasta in plenty of salted water, drain and mix with the clam sauce. Serve piping hot.

Pasta with fried courgettes
Pasta c'a cucuzza fritta

- 400 g (16 oz) trenette pasta
- 1 courgette for frying
- 200 g (8 oz) olive oil
- 1 sprig of basil
- caciocavallo or parmesan cheese
- pasta cooking water
- salt and pepper or ground chilli

In a little frying pan, deep fry the courgettes in olive oil, after having cut them into approximately 1/2 cm (1/4 inch) thick roundels, and then set aside, reserving a little of the oil. Cook the pasta, and drain off reserving just a few tablespoons of the cooking water. Serve "al dente" with one tablespoon of the oil used for frying the courgettes and one tablespoon of the pasta cooking water per serving. Garnish with a few basil leaves, pepper or ground chilli and lots of grated cheese.

Variation: instead of the courgettes, fried aubergine slices may be used.

Baked lasagne with meat

- 12 sheets of fresh lasagne

For the sauce:
- 1 carrot
- 1 onion
- 2 celery stalks
- 2 dl (6 fl oz) olive oil
- 400 g (16 oz) minced beef
- 1 dl (3 fl oz) white wine
- 150 g (6 oz) tomato puree
- salt and pepper
- water

For the béchamel sauce:
- 1 l (32 fl oz) milk
- 150 g (6 oz) butter
- 100 g (4 oz) flour
- salt
- a pinch of nutmeg

In a pot, cook the pasta sheets, drain and pass them through cold water.

In a saucepan, boil 3/4 of the milk with salt, nutmeg and butter. In a bowl, dissolve the flour in the remaining 1/4 of milk. When the milk starts boiling, add the dissolved flour mixture and cook until it starts to thicken.

In another saucepan, sauté the chopped carrot, onion and celery in the oil; add the mince meat. Add a few dashes of wine and then the tomato puree, dilute with the water, finally add a little salt and pepper and cook for about 15 minutes over a moderate heat.

Grease a rectangular baking dish with butter, cover with a thin layer of béchamel sauce and put 4 sheets of pasta over it. Spread out a layer of béchamel and a few spoonfuls of meat sauce here and there. Cover with more sheets of pasta; repeat, alternating the ingredients until all the pasta has been used. Finish with a layer of béchamel and meat sauce. Bake in a pre-heated 150°C (300°F) oven for about 15 minutes. Leave to cool before serving.

Pasta timbale with sardines

- 400 g (16 oz) maccheroncelli pasta
- 2 sachets of saffron

For the sauce:
- 1 bunch of wild fennel
- 1 onion
- 4 anchovy fillets
- 2 dl (6 fl oz) olive oil
- 100 g (4 oz) raisins and pine nuts
- salt and pepper
- 300 g (12 oz) fresh, boned sardines
- fennel cooking water
- breadcrumbs

Prepare the sauce in the same way as for "Pasta with sardines".

Cook the pasta, drain and mix with half of the sauce and a little olive oil.

In the meantime, oil a round baking dish and coat with breadcrumbs. Put half of the pasta mixed with the sauce into the baking dish and form a shallow, slightly hollowed layer. Pour the rest of the sauce over and cover with the remaining pasta. Oil the top part and sprinkle with breadcrumbs. Bake in a pre-heated 150°C (300°F) oven for about 15 minutes. Leave to cool for a few minutes before turning out.

Sicilian pasta timbale

- 400 g (16 oz) of anelletti pasta

For the sauce:
- 1 carrot
- 1 onion
- 2 celery stalks
- 300 g (12 oz) tomato puree
- water
- olive oil

For the filling:
- 1 carrot
- 1 onion
- 2 celery stalks
- 600 g (24 oz) minced beef
- 200 g (8 oz) peas
- a dash of white wine
- 150 g (6 oz) tomato puree
- 150 g (6 oz) fresh caciocavallo cheese
- olive oil and breadcrumbs
- 1 aubergine (optional)
- salt and pepper
- water

In a saucepan, sauté the chopped carrot, celery and onion in the oil, and add the tomato puree.

Dilute with water, correct the salt, add a little pepper, then cook for about 15 minutes.

In a separate saucepan, sauté the other chopped carrot, celery and onion in the oil, add the minced beef and peas and cook until brown. Add a few dashes of wine and then the tomato puree. Dilute with enough water to form a dense filling, add salt, pepper, and cook over a moderate heat for about 20 minutes.

Fry the diced aubergine and dice the caciocavallo cheese.

Oil a round baking dish and coat with the breadcrumbs.

Boil the anelletti in plenty of salted water. Drain and mix with the sauce and, if desired, with grated caciocavallo cheese. Put half of the pasta mixed with the sauce in the baking dish and form a shallow, slightly hollowed layer; evenly distribute the carrot mixture, the aubergines and the diced caciocavallo cheese. Cover with the other half of the pasta, drizzle a little oil over and sprinkle with breadcrumbs. Bake in a pre-heated 150°C (300°F) oven for about 15 minutes. Finally, remove the timbale from the oven, leave to cool a little and then turn out.

Roast lamb
Agneddu 'nfurnatu

- 1.5 kg (3 lbs) lamb, cut in large pieces
- 2 dl (6 fl oz) olive oil
- a pinch of pepper or crumbled chilli
- a pinch of salt
- 3 dl (9 fl oz) diluted meat extract
- 2 garlic cloves (optional)
- 2 dl (6 fl oz) white wine

Pour the oil with the spices into a baking dish. Arrange the lamb and bake in the oven for about 30 minutes. Remove from the oven, add a few dashes of wine, and the meat extract, put it back in the oven and cook for a further 30 minutes. Serve hot, with potatoes baked with rosemary on the side.

Variation: kid meat may be used instead of lamb.

Stewed lamb
Agneddu aggrassatu

- 1.5 kg (3 lbs) lamb, cut in large pieces
- 2 dl (6 fl oz) olive oil
- 2 onions
- 3 dl (9 fl oz) white wine
- 3 dl (9 fl oz) diluted meat extract
- a pinch of salt and pepper
- water

In a saucepan, brown the sliced onion in oil, add the lamb and cook over a low heat for about 5 minutes. Pour in the wine, the meat extract and the water. Add salt and pepper, cover the saucepan and continue cooking for another 50 minutes or so over a moderate heat. Serve piping hot.

Variation: sage, rosemary and a garlic clove may be added.

Steak in a vinegar and oregano dressing
Arrustu all'argintera

- 4 sirloin steaks weighing 200 g (8 oz) each
- 1 dl (3 fl oz) olive oil
- 4 whole garlic cloves
- 1 dl (3 fl oz) wine vinegar
- 200 g (8 oz) breadcrumbs
- oregano
- a pinch of salt

Grease the meat with olive oil and coat with bread-crumbs. In a frying pan, brown the whole garlic cloves in half of the oil, add the meat and, when it is almost cooked, remove the cooking oil, and add the remaining oil. Add a few dashes of vinegar, then sprinkle with oregano and salt. Serve piping hot with the cooking juice.

Palermo-style steak
Arrustu 'mpanatu

- 4 sirloin steaks weighing 200 g (8 oz) each
- 300 g (12 oz) breadcrumbs
- 2 garlic cloves, finely chopped
- olive oil
- a pinch of salt
- oregano

Mix the breadcrumbs, oregano, salt and garlic in a bowl. Grease the meat with olive oil and coat with the breadcrumb mixture. Cook on both sides over a red-hot grill. Serve hot, adding a little more salt if necessary, and a drizzle of oil.

Variation: marinate the meat in a mixture of oil, lemon, salt, pepper and oregano for at least a couple of hours. Grill for a few minutes on both sides, then pour the marinade over and serve hot.

Veal steaks
Braciolittina

- 800 g (32 oz) veal boneless rump steaks
- 2 onions
- 2 dl (6 fl oz) white wine
- 2 dl (6 fl oz) olive oil
- 2 dl (6 fl oz) diluted meat extract
- a pinch of salt and pepper
- 1 sprig of parsley

Brown the thinly sliced onion in the oil. Add the meat and cook for approximately 5 minutes. Moisten with the wine and the meat extract. Add salt and pepper and cook over a moderate heat for a further 5 minutes. Serve hot with lots of finely chopped parsley.

Sweet and sour rabbit
Cunigghiu all'agroduci

- 1 rabbit, cut into pieces
- 2 onions
- 100 g (4 oz) sugar
- 4 dl (12 fl oz) wine vinegar
- a pinch of salt
- 1 sprig parsley, finely chopped
- 2 dl (6 fl oz) olive oil

In a pan, lightly fry the thinly sliced onion in the oil, add the rabbit and cook for about 5 minutes.
Add the vinegar, the sugar and dilute with water. Add a little salt and cook for about an hour over a moderate heat.
Sprinkle with finely chopped parsley and serve hot.

* photo

Sweet and sour rabbit with green olives and capers
Cunigghiu apparecchiatu

- 1 rabbit, cut into large pieces
- flour
- 200 g (8 oz) pitted green olives
- 50 g (2 oz) capers
- 25 g (1 oz) sugar
- 1 onion
- 2 celery stalks
- 2 dl (6 fl oz) vinegar
- 200 g (8 oz) peeled tomatoes
- 2 dl (6 fl oz) olive oil
- salt and pepper

Dust the pieces of rabbit with flour and sear over a moderate heat until golden brown all over. Add the vinegar and sugar, correct the salt, add pepper and cook for a few more minutes covered with the lid.
In another pan, sauté the coarsely chopped onion, the blanched celery, capers and olives. Add the tomatoes and when the ingredients are well blended pour over the rabbit. Cook for about 40 minutes. Serve cold.

Stewed rabbit
Cunigghiu a stufatu

- 1 rabbit, cut into pieces
- 2 dl (6 fl oz) olive oil
- 2 onions
- 2 dl (6 fl oz) white wine
- a pinch of salt and pepper
- 200 g (8 oz) peeled tomatoes
- water

Sautéé the finely sliced onions in oil. Add the rabbit and cook over a low heat for about 5 minutes. Add a few dashes of wine and then the peeled tomatoes. Let the meat soak up the flavour, dilute the sauce with water, add salt and pepper and cook over a moderate heat for further 50 minutes. Serve hot.

Rabbit in red wine
Cunigghiu cu vinu russu

- 1 rabbit, cut into pieces
- 1 onion
- 2 celery stalks
- 1 carrot
- 2 dl (6 fl oz) olive oil

- 1 dl (3 fl oz) full red wine
- 2 dl (6 fl oz) diluted meat extract
- a pinch of salt and pepper
- water, if required

Sautéé the chopped onion, celery and carrot in the oil. Add the rabbit and cook for about 10 minutes. Add the wine and the diluted meat extract. Correct the salt, add pepper, and cook for about an hour. Check the cooking juice, if it has dried up add some water. Serve hot.

Grilled lamb cutlets
Custateddi d'agneddu arrustuti

- 16 lamb cutlets
- a pinch of salt
- a pinch of pepper

Tenderise the cutlets, add salt, pepper, then grill over a moderate heat for about 10 minutes. Serve hot with lemon wedges on the side.

Variation: kid meat may be cooked following the same rocedure.

Breaded pork steaks
Porcu a cotoletta

- 4 pork steaks weighing about 100 g (4 oz) each, well tenderised
- white flour
- 1 egg
- 200 g (8 oz) breadcrumbs
- 1 dl (3 fl oz) wine vinegar
- a pinch of salt
- vegetable oil

Marinate the meat in the vinegar for a couple of hours. Drain, dust with flour, dip in the beaten egg with a little salt added, and then coat with breadcrumbs. Fry in hot oil on both sides. Serve hot with lemon wedges on the side.

Variation: chicken breasts, and turkey or veal steaks may be cooked following the same procedure.

Pork chops with black olives
Custateddi di porcu cu l'alivi nivuri

- 4 pork chops weighing 200 g (8 oz) each
- 2 dl (6 fl oz) olive oil
- 100 g (4 oz) pitted black olives
- 100 g (4 oz) butter
- 1 dl (3 fl oz) white wine
- 1 dl (3 fl oz) diluted meat extract

In a frying pan, brown the chops in the oil over a low heat. Remove the fat, add the butter and olives, pour in the wine and finally the diluted meat extract. Cook until the sauce is well blended then serve hot.

Breaded heart
Cori 'mpanatu

- 800 g (32 oz) sliced heart
- olive oil
- breadcrumbs
- a pinch of salt

Grease the meat with oil, add salt and coat with breadcrumbs. Arrange in a frying pan and cook for about 10 minutes. Serve with a drizzle of oil.

Stuffed meat roll

- 1 very thin slice of beef weighing approx. 600 g (24 oz)
- 200 g (8 oz) minced beef
- 150 g (6 oz) grated caciocavallo or pecorino cheese
- 2 hard boiled eggs
- 100 g (4 oz) breadcrumbs
- 1 onion
- 2 dl (6 fl oz) red wine
- olive oil
- a pinch of salt and pepper
- water

Spread the meat out carefully on the work top, cover with cling-film and lightly tenderise it. Put the mince meat into a bowl and mix with the grated cheese, breadcrumbs, salt and pepper until the ingredients are well blended. Spread the mixture out on one side of the slice of beef and put the sliced hard boiled eggs on top.
Roll up the meat and tie with kitchen string.

In a large pan, brown the onion with the oil, then add the meat, searing it for about 2 minutes. Pour in the wine and dilute the cooking juice with two glasses of water.
Cook over a moderate heat for a good half an hour.
Leave to cool. Remove the string and cut the meat roll into 2 cm (3/4 inch) thick slices. Pour the meat juices over the meat and serve.

Palermo-style Liver
Ficatu a palermitana

- 4 slices of veal liver weighing 200 g (8 oz) each
- breadcrumbs
- 2 garlic cloves, minced
- a pinch of salt
- a pinch of oregano
- olive oil

In a bowl, mix the breadcrumbs, salt, oregano and finely chopped garlic.
Brush the liver with oil and coat with the breadcrumb mixture on both sides. Place on the red-hot griddle and cook over a moderate heat for about 10 minutes. Serve hot with a drizzle of oil.

* photo

Sweet and sour Liver
Ficatu all'agroduci

- 800 g (32 oz) veal liver
- 2 onions
- 2 dl (6 fl oz) wine vinegar

- 100 g (4 oz) sugar
- a pinch of salt
- 1dl (3 fl oz) olive oil

In a frying pan, brown the onions cut into rondels in the oil. Add the thinly sliced liver and cook over a moderate heat for about 5 minutes, turning each slice. Add the sugar, after dissolving it in the vinegar. Correct the salt and serve hot.

Variation: coat the thinly sliced liver with breadcrumbs and fry. Arrange in a dish and sprinkle with mint leaves and finely chopped garlic. Reserve one or two tablespoons of the fried oil in the pan and add the vinegar and the sugar. When the sugar has dissolved pour over the liver. Serve cold.

Chicken drumsticks
Gammunedda di gaddina

- 12 chicken drumsticks
- 500 g (1 lb) fresh peas, shelled
- 2 dl (6 fl oz) olive oil
- 1 onion
- 1 sachet of saffron
- water
- a pinch of salt and pepper

In an earthenware pot, brown the onion cut into rondels in the oil. Add the peas, saffron and water. Correct the salt, add a little pepper and continue cooking for about 10 minutes. In a frying pan, sear the chicken drumsticks. Once golden brown, add them to the peas, cover with a lid and cook over a moderate heat for about 20 minutes. Serve hot.

Variation: meatballs or roulades may be cooked in the same way (see the recipe "Roulades in sauce").

Palermo-style top round
Lacerto aggrassatu a palermitana

- 1 kg (2 lbs) top round of veal
- 2 white onions
- 3 dl (9 fl oz) dry white wine
- 2 dl (6 fl oz) olive oil
- 1 tbsp tomato puree
- 1 sprig of rosemary
- 3 crumbled bay leaves
- a pinch of salt and pepper

Sauté the finely sliced onions in half of the oil over a moderate heat. Place the meat and spices into a saucepan. Sear evenly. Add the cooked onions and tomato puree, pour in the wine, add salt and pepper and cook for about 90 minutes. Remove and slice the meat. Mash the onion sauce with a wooden spoon until creamy. If necessary, add a knob of butter and pour over the meat. Serve hot.

Variation: lean pork or chicken may be used in place of the veal.
Moreover, the sauce may be used with spaghetti or linguine cooked "al dente". In this case, sprinkle the pasta with parmesan cheese.

Calf gristle salad

- 600 g (24 oz) calf gristle (muzzle and jaw)
- 2 lemons
- olive oil
- a pinch of salt and pepper

Buy the cooked muzzle and jaw at the butcher's. Place on a serving dish. Add oil, lemon, salt and pepper. Toss and serve cold after leaving to rest for a couple of hours.

Variation: chopped tomato, pitted green olives, thinly sliced celery, or anything else desired may be added.

Roulades
Bruciulittina

- 16 thin slices of veal weighing 30 g (1 oz) each
- 100 g (4 oz) mortadella
- 100 g (4 oz) ham
- 100 g (4 oz) Neapolitan-style salami
- 100 g (4 oz) fresh caciocavallo cheese
- 10 slices of sandwich loaf bread
- 3 eggs
- bay leaves
- onions cut in wedges
- olive oil
- salt

Dice the cold meat, cheese and bread. Put them into a bowl, add the eggs and mix until well blended. Place a little of the mixture on each slice of meat. Roll the meat up, folding in at the ends to stop the filling from running out while being cooked. On long wooden skewers, thread a meat roulade, a bay leaf, an onion wedge, then another roulade, etc.. Brush with oil and coat with breadcrumbs. Grill over a moderate heat for about 10 minutes. Serve hot with a drizzle of oil.

Variation: for a different filling, mix an equal amount of breadcrumbs and parmesan or caciocavallo cheese, add the oil in which a small onion and finely chopped parsley have been sautéed. The roulades may also be baked in the oven or pan cooked. In this case, add a little oil and a dash of dry white wine.

Roulades in sauce
Bruciulittina a ragù

- 8 slices of veal weighing 100 g (4 oz) each
- 2 onions
- 100 g (4 oz) pine nuts
- 100 g (4 oz) raisins
- 100 g (4 oz) peeled tomatoes
- 2 dl (6 fl oz) olive oil
- 100 g (4 oz) grated caciocavallo cheese
- 100 g (4 oz) fresh caciocavallo cheese
- a pinch of salt
- a sandwich bread loaf
- 2 celery stalks
- 2 carrots
- 1 dl (3 fl oz) dry white wine
- 300 g (12 oz) tomato puree
- water
- a pinch of pepper

In a bowl, mix the crumbled bread, a pinch of salt, and the grated cheese. In a frying pan, brown the onion in oil, add the raisins and pine nuts. Add to the bread mixture together with the peeled tomatoes and the diced fresh caciocavallo cheese. Mix well so that the ingredients are well blended. Tenderise the slices of meat and put a spoon-ful of the cheese mixture in the middle. Roll the meat up, folding in the ends to stop the filling from running out when being cooked. Tie with thin kitchen string or use a toothpick to close the ends.

Prepare the sauce by sautéing the chopped onion, carrot and celery in the oil. Add the tomato puree and dilute with water. Add salt and pepper and cook for 10 minutes over a moderate heat. In a little frying pan, sear the roulades in a drizzle of oil and then add a dash of wine. When they are golden brown, add to the sauce and cook for other 10 minutes.

Serve hot, coated with the sauce.

Boiled beef
Carni vugghiuta

- 1 kg (2 lbs) beef
- 2 celery stalks
- 2 onions
- 5 carrots
- 5 ripe tomatoes
- a pinch of salt
- water
- 2 dl (6 fl oz) of Marsala (optional)

Put the meat into a pot. Add the finely chopped carrots, celery, tomatoes and onion. Cover with water and boil for about an hour over a moderate heat. Correct the salt, and if desired, add the Marsala. Serve hot with the cooking stock.

Mixed pork meat in sauce
Porcu a ragù

- 4 sausages
- 500 g (1 lb) pork rind
- 300 g (12 oz) pork chops
- 400 g (16 oz) tomato puree
- 1 dl (3 fl oz) olive oil
- 2 carrots
- 2 celery stalks
- 1 onion
- water
- a pinch of salt and pepper
- 15 g (0.5 oz) fennel seeds
- 2 dl (6 fl oz) white wine

In an earthenware pan, sauté for about 2 minutes the finely chopped onion, celery, carrots in the oil. Add the chops and chopped pork rind and lightly brown them. Pour in the wine and wait for a few minutes before stirring in the diluted tomato puree. Add enough water to produce a medium density liquid. Correct the salt, add pepper and cook for 15 minutes together with the fennel seeds being careful not to let the sauce thicken too much. In this case, adjust the quantity of water. Cut the sausages into little pieces and add to the sauce. Cook for a further 10 minutes. Serve piping hot.

Variation: for less fat content, leave out the pork rind and double the amount of chops.

Sicilian Cooking

Chicken with tomatoes
Gaddu cu u pummaroru

- 1 chicken, cut up into pieces
- 4 ripe tomatoes, peeled and seeded
- 1 onion
- 1 garlic clove
- 2 dl (6 fl oz) olive oil
- a pinch of salt and pepper
- basil or parsley, finely chopped
- 2 dl (6 fl oz) white wine

Brown the chicken with the sliced onion, garlic in oil. Add the tomatoes, salt and pepper, and pour in the wine. Cook for about 30 minutes over a low heat, turning the chicken over to stop it from sticking to the pan. If necessary, add a few tablespoons of water. Serve hot, sprinkled with fresh basil or finely chopped parsley.

Variation: add 4 yellow and green peppers chopped and cooked in oil and a little water. Alternatively, 100 g (4 oz) of black pitted olives and a pinch of oregano may be added to the sauce.

Fried meatballs
Purpetti fritti

- 800 g (32 oz) minced beef
- 1 onion
- 6 slices of sandwich loaf bread
- 1.5 dl (5 fl oz) milk
- 150 g (6 oz) grated caciocavallo cheese
- 3 eggs
- a sprig of parsley, finely chopped
- a pinch of salt and pepper
- vegetable and olive oil

In a bowl, mix the minced meat, the finely chopped onion, the bread slices soaked in milk, the cheese, the parsley, salt and pepper, and the eggs until all the ingredients are well blended. Using the mixture, form little balls, flatten slightly and then deep fry. Serve hot.

Variation: put the fried meatballs into fresh tomato sauce, cook for a few minutes and garnish with fresh basil leaves.

Meatballs in sauce
Purpetti a ragù

- 800 g (32 oz) minced beef
- 2 onions
- 8 slices of sandwich loaf bread
- 2 dl (6 fl oz) milk
- 150 g (6 oz) grated parmesan cheese
- a pinch of salt and pepper
- 3 eggs
- a sprig of parsley, finely chopped
- vegetable oil for frying
- 2 dl (6 fl oz) olive oil
- 2 celery stalks
- 2 carrots
- 300 g (12 oz) tomato puree
- 2 dl (6 fl oz) white wine
- water
- a pinch of nutmeg

In a bowl, mix the meat, the eggs, a little pepper, a pinch of salt, the finely chopped parsley, the bread soaked in milk, the parmesan cheese and the nutmeg until well blended.

Shape into medallions weighing approx. 40 g (2 oz) each. Fry for a few minutes in vegetable oil, add the wine and let it evaporate. Add them to the sauce prepared by sautéing, in a saucepan, the finely chopped onion, carrots, and celery in the oil. Add the tomato puree and dilute with water. Add a pinch of salt and pepper and cook for about 15 minutes. Serve hot.

Meat loaf
Purpittuni

- 1 kg (2 lbs) minced beef
- 1 onion
- 5 slices of sandwich loaf bread
- 1 dl (3 fl oz) milk
- 150 g (6 oz) grated cacio-cavallo cheese
- 250 g (1/2 lb) fresh cacio-cavallo cheese
- 150 g (6 oz) ham
- a pinch of salt

In a bowl, mix the meat, the bread soaked in milk, the grated cheese and salt until the ingredients are well blended. Put the mixture onto a sheet of greased tinfoil, and form it a large oblong shape. Using your fingers make a sort of groove to be filled with the fresh caciocavallo cheese, the onion and the ham cut into strips. Close the edges of the mixture back together again and roll in the tinfoil. Bake in a pre-heated 180°C (350°F) oven for about 15 minutes. Remove from the oven, leave to rest for about 10 minutes, slice and serve.

Palermo-style sausages
Sasizza a palermitana

- 12 sausages
- 200 g (8 oz) breadcrumbs
- a pinch of oregano
- olive oil
- 2 garlic cloves, finely chopped

With a sharp knife, cut the sausages in half lengthways. Open them up and oil on both sides. Coat with the breadcrumbs seasoned with garlic and oregano. Cook on a red-hot grill on both sides. Serve piping hot with a drizzle of oil.

Sausages in white wine
Sasizza fritta cu vinu

- 12 pork sausages
- 1 dl (3 fl oz) olive oil
- 50 g (2 oz) margarine

- 1 dl (3 fl oz) white wine
- water
- 2 dl (6 fl oz) diluted meat extract

Give the sausages a wheel shape, thread with the metal or wooden skewers and prick with a fork. Put the wheel into a frying pan and cover with water. Cook over a moderate heat for about 10 minutes. Remove the water, add the oil and margarine, and brown on both sides. Add the white wine and the meat extract and cook for a further 5 minutes or so.

* photo

"Conca d'oro" escalopes
Sgaloppina a la conca d'oru

- 8 slices of rump of veal weighing about 70 g (3 oz) each
- 8 slices of aubergine
- 8 processed cheese slices
- 50 g (2 oz) fresh tomato sauce
- 1 dl (3 fl oz) olive oil
- 50 g (2 oz) margarine
- a pinch of salt
- basil leaves

In a frying pan, brown the slices of meat on both sides in the oil and margarine, sprinkling them with a little salt. Fry the aubergines separately and put one on top of each slice of meat. Cover with the cheese slices, bake in the oven until the cheese melts, then pour a dash of tomato sauce over each escalope. Serve piping hot garnished with basil leaves.

Lemon escalopes
Sgaloppina cu limiuni

- 8 slices of rump of veal weighing about 70 g (3 oz) each
- 1 dl (3 fl oz) olive oil
- 100 g (4 oz) margarine
- juice of 4 lemons
- a pinch of salt and pepper

In a frying pan, brown the slices of meat on both sides in oil and in half of the margarine. Remove the fat and add the other half of the margarine and the lemon juice. Correct the salt, add pepper to taste and serve hot with the cooking juice.

Variation: to prepare a dish with less fat, lightly dust the meat with flour and brown in oil, add the lemon juice, salt and pepper and then a knob of butter before serving.

Marsala escalopes
Sgaloppina cu a Marsala

- 8 slices of rump of veal weighing about 70 g (30 g) each
- 1 dl (3 fl oz) olive oil
- 100 g (4 oz) margarine
- 1 dl (3 fl oz) Marsala
- salt
- 2 dl (6 fl oz) diluted meat extract

Brown the slices of meat on both sides in a frying pan with the oil and half the amount of margarine. Remove the fat from the pan and add the diluted meat extract and the other half of the margarine. Add a few dashes of Marsala. Cook for about 5 minutes.

Variation: see the procedure suggested in the variation for "Lemon escalopes".

Kid meat stew with potatoes
Spizzatinu di crapettu cu i patati

- 1.5 kg (3 lbs) kid meat, cut into large pieces
- 1 kg (2 lbs) potatoes, cut into large pieces
- 2 onions
- 2 dl (6 fl oz) olive oil
- 2 dl (6 fl oz) white wine
- water
- a pinch of salt and pepper
- a sachet of saffron

In a saucepan, brown the sliced onion in oil, add the kid meat and cook over a moderate for a further 5 minutes. Pour in the wine, the saffron and the water; after other 5 minutes add the potatoes.

Add salt and pepper and cook for a further 40 minutes or so until the meat and potatoes are well cooked and a creamy sauce has formed. Serve hot.

Beef stew with potatoes
Spizzatinu cu li patati

- 1 kg (2 lbs) beef, coarsely diced
- 2 onions
- 2 dl (6 fl oz) olive oil
- 2 dl (6 fl oz) dry white wine
- 50 g (2 oz) tomato puree
- a pinch of salt and pepper
- 1 kg (2 lbs) potatoes, coarsely diced

Slice the onion and lightly sauté with the oil in a large saucepan. Add the meat and brown for about 5 minutes. Pour in the wine, then add the tomato puree diluted with water, salt and pepper. Cook over a moderate heat for about 30 minutes. Add the potatoes and, if necessary, a little more water. Cook for another 30 minutes until the potatoes become creamy. Serve hot.

Meat and citron kebabs
Spitini di capuliatu

- 600 g (24 oz) minced beef
- 4 slices of sandwich loaf bread
- 100 g (4 oz) grated parmesan cheese
- zest of 1 citron, finely chopped
- juice of 5 citrons
- 150 g (6 oz) butter
- 2 dl (6 fl oz) olive oil
- 150 g (6 oz) margarine
- citron leaves
- salt
- 2 eggs

In a bowl, mix the minced meat, the crumbled bread, cheese, citron zest, a pinch of salt and the eggs until well blended. Form little meatballs and thread onto a skewer alternating with the citron leaves.

In a frying pan, melt the margarine in the oil. Brown the meat kebabs over a moderate heat for about 12 minutes. When almost cooked, remove the fat and add the butter and citron juice. Cook for a further two minutes making sure that the butter does not burn. Serve hot with the citron sauce.

Grilled mixed kebabs
Spitini arrustuti

- 5 sausages
- 400 g (16 oz) lean pork
- 200 g (8 oz) smoked bacon
- 200 g (8 oz) fresh peppers
- 200 g (8 oz) veal liver
- a pinch of salt and pepper

Dice all the ingredients into 3-4 cm (1-1.5 inch) pieces. Thread onto wooden skewers alternating the ingredients.
Lay the kebabs on a grill brushed with oil, add salt and cook for about 15 minutes over a moderate heat, turning often. Serve hot.

Baked pork shins
Coscia di porcu a furnu

- 4 pork shins
- 3 dl (9 fl oz) diluted meat extract
- 1 dl (3 fl oz) olive oil
- a dash of white wine
- a pinch of salt and pepper
- a twig of rosemary

Make little cuts in the shins with a sharp knife and fill with the spices.
Arrange the meat in a greased baking dish and bake for about 20 minutes. Add a few dashes of wine and the diluted meat extract, and cook for a further 10 minutes. Serve hot.

Olivetan-style tripe
Trippa all'alivitana

- 600 g (24 oz) tripe
- 2 onions
- 2 dl (6 fl oz) olive oil
- 300 g (12 oz) peeled tomatoes
- 150 g (6 oz) grated caciocavallo cheese
- 100 g (4 oz) breadcrumbs
- a pinch of salt and pepper
- water

In a saucepan, sauté the chopped onion in the oil. Add the tripe cut into strips and cook for about 10 minutes over a low heat. Add the peeled tomatoes and dilute with a little water. Cook for a further 5 minutes. As soon as the tripe starts to dry out, add the cheese, salt and pepper. Stir for a few minutes, then sprinkle with toasted breadcrumbs. Serve hot.

Variation: instead of caciocavallo cheese and breadcrumbs, use parmesan cheese and garnish with basil leaves.

Fried albacore
Alalonga fritta

- 4 albacore steaks weighing 200 g (8 oz) each
- olive oil
- a pinch of salt
- strong flour

Heat the oil in a frying pan, add the lightly floured fish steaks and cook for about 5 minutes on both sides. Place on kitchen paper to remove the excess oil. Add salt and serve hot with lemon wedges on the side.

Grilled yellowtail

- 4 yellowtail steaks weighing 200 g (8 oz) each
- 1 dl (3 fl oz) olive oil
- a pinch of salt
- a sprig of parsley, finely chopped

Brush the fish steaks with oil, add salt and place them on a red-hot grill. Cook on both sides over a moderate heat. Serve hot with a drizzle of oil and finely chopped parsley.

Sweet and sour salt cod
Baccalaru in agro e duci

- 800 g (32 oz) salt cod, desalted and cut into pieces
- 2 onions
- 2 dl (6 fl oz) vinegar
- 50 g (2 oz) sugar
- water
- 6 dl (18 fl oz) olive oil
- a sprig of parsley, finely chopped
- strong flour
- salt

Boil the salt cod for 10 minutes, remove the skin and bones and then dust with flour. Pour the oil into a frying pan, add the fish and fry for about 10 minutes on both sides. Arrange the fish in a serving dish. In another pan, cook the onion in salted water until it becomes soft and transparent, add the sugar and, when dissolved, add a dash of vinegar. Pour the sauce onto the serving dish, garnish with chopped parsley and serve cold.

Fried salt cod
Baccalaru frittu

- 800 g (32 oz) salt cod, desalted
- strong flour
- olive oil
- a pinch of salt

Blanch the salt cod, remove the skin and bones, cut into pieces and dust with flour. Heat the oil in a frying pan and add the pieces of fish. Fry for about 12 minutes or so over a moderate heat. Serve hot, after having removed the excess oil with kitchen paper, and sprinkle with salt.

Salt cod baked in tomato sauce
Baccalaru a sfinciuni

- 800 g (32 oz) salt cod, cut into pieces
- 3 onions
- 4 dl (12 fl oz) olive oil
- 200 g (8 oz) tomato puree
- 50 g (2 oz) anchovy fillets

- 100 g (4 oz) breadcrumbs
- a pinch of salt and pepper
- a sprig of parsley
- 1 dl (3 fl oz) vinegar
- water

Boil the salt cod in water flavoured with vinegar and parsley. Drain and remove the skin and bones, then put it into a greased baking dish.
In a frying pan, brown the finely chopped onion in the oil, add the anchovy fillets making sure that they dissolve, and then the tomato puree. Dilute with a little water and add salt and pepper.
Cook for about 15 minutes over a moderate heat until the sauce has thickened slightly. Pour it evenly over the salt cod in the baking dish. Sprinkle the top with breadcrumbs and bake in a pre-heated 180°C (350°F) oven for about 12 minutes. Serve warm with fresh, finely chopped parsley.

* photo

Fried squid
Calamari fritti

- 4 squid weighing 300 g (12 oz) each
- strong flour
- olive oil
- a pinch of salt

Empty the squids, removing the internal cartilage. Cut into rings and dust with flour. Deep fry in olive oil.
Serve hot sprinkled with salt and garnish with lemon wedges on the side.

Lipari-style squid
Calamari a' liparota

- 4 squid weighing 300 g (12 oz) each
- 1 onion
- 2 dl (6 fl oz) olive oil
- 2 dl (6 fl oz) white wine
- 1 sachet of saffron

- 30 g (1 oz) desalted capers
- a pinch of salt and pepper
- water
- a sprig of parsley, finely chopped

Empty the squid, remove the internal cartilage and cut into rings. In a saucepan, sauté the chopped onion in the oil, add the squid and brown for 5 minutes. Pour in the wine, add the capers and the saffron. Dilute the cooking juice with water, add salt, pepper and cook for a further 12 minutes. Serve hot with the cooking juice and plenty of finely chopped parsley.

* photo

Stuffed squid
Calamari chini

- 4 squid weighing 300 g (12 oz) each
- 13 slices of sandwich loaf bread
- 50 g (2 oz) raisins and pine nuts
- 100 g (4 oz) grated parmesan cheese
- 3 eggs
- a sprig of parsley, finely chopped
- 4 garlic cloves
- 400 g (16 oz) peeled tomatoes
- 2 dl (6 fl oz) olive oil
- 1 sprig of fresh mint leaves
- salt
- 2 onions

Empty and skin the squid putting the tentacles aside to be used later for the filling. In a bowl, mix the crumbled bread with the parmesan cheese, a pinch of salt and the finely chopped parsley. In a frying pan, brown one chopped onion, the tentacles cut into pieces, the raisins and pine nuts. After a few minutes pour into the bowl with the bread mixture, adding also the eggs. Mix thoroughly until well blended. Fill the squid with the mixture and close them with a toothpick. In a saucepan, brown the remaining onion in the oil, add the tomatoes, salt, pepper, and the mint leaves. Cook for 10 minutes. Brown the squid separately in a little oil. Add them to the tomato sauce and cook for a further 20 minutes over a moderate heat. Serve cold along with the tomato sauce.

Baked dusky sea perch with black olives
Cernia e alivi nivuri 'nfurnati

- 4 dusky sea perch steaks weighing 200 g (8 oz) each
- 6 garlic cloves
- 200 g (8 oz) of pitted black olives
- 2 dl (6 fl oz) white wine
- 2 dl (6 fl oz) olive oil
- a pinch of salt and pepper

In a baking dish, fry the garlic cloves in oil and remove as soon as they start to turn brown. Arrange the fish steaks, add salt, pepper and the wine. Add the olives and bake in a pre-heated 150°C (300°F) oven for 10 minutes.

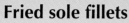

Fried sole fillets
Linguata fritta

- 8 soles, weighing 200 g (8 oz) each
- olive oil
- a good pinch of salt
- strong flour

Clean and gut the sole, then remove the skin. With a knife, separate the fillets working along the central line. Dust with flour and place in a frying pan with hot oil, leaving them to cook for 5 minutes over a low flame. Serve hot sprinkled with salt.

Grilled prawns
Gammaruna arrustuti

- 40 medium-sized prawns
- olive oil
- a pinch of salt
- a sprig of parsley, finely chopped

Thread the prawns onto wooden skewers. Brush them with oil, add salt, place on the grill and cook for about 5 minutes on both sides. Serve hot with a drizzle of oil and finely chopped parsley.

Breaded prawns
Gammaruna a cotoletta

- 40 prawns
- white flour
- 3 eggs
- breadcrumbs
- a pinch of salt
- olive oil

Peel the prawns, and dust with flour, dip in the beaten eggs and coat with bread-crumbs. Heat the oil in a frying pan and add the prawns. Brown them for about 5 minutes turning them over. Serve hot with a pinch of salt.

Swordfish roulades
Bruciulittina di pisci spata

- 12 thin slices of swordfish weighing 30 g (1 oz) each
- 200 g (8 oz) swordfish flesh
- 10 slices of sandwich loaf bread
- 2 onions
- 2 dl (6 fl oz) olive oil
- 100 g (4 oz) raisins and pine nuts
- 3 eggs
- 100 g (4 oz) grated parmesan cheese
- a sprig of parsley, finely chopped
- a pinch of salt
- 16 bay leaves

Crumble the bread and put it into a bowl along with the cheese, parsley and salt. Finely chop the onion, and sauté in a frying pan. Add the raisins, pine nuts, and the diced fish and cook for about 5 minutes.

Pour the mixture into the bowl with the bread and mix thoroughly, adding the eggs, until all the ingredients are well blended. Flatten the slices of fish and put a little of the filling in the middle of each slice. Roll carefully, making sure that they are well closed.

Thread onto wooden skewers alternating with slices of onion and bay leaves. Brush with oil, and coat with breadcrumbs. Grill on both sides for about 12 minutes over a moderate heat. Serve piping hot with a drizzle of oil.

Breaded codling
Mirruzzedda a cotoletta

- 6 codling weighing 150 g (6 oz) each
- 3 eggs
- 200 g (8 oz) breadcrumbs
- white flour
- white wine vinegar
- vegetable and olive oil
- a pinch of salt

Clean the codling, open them up like a book, wash thoroughly, and arrange in a bowl, covering them with vinegar. Marinate for 3 hours.
Drain well, dust with flour, dip in the beaten egg with a pinch of salt, and coat with breadcrumbs. Fry in hot vegetable oil mixed with a couple of spoons of olive oil. Serve hot.

Variation: mackerel of the same weight may used instead of the codling.

Swordfish in sauce
Pisci spata a brodettu

- 4 swordfish steaks weighing 200 g (8 oz) each
- 2 dl (6 fl oz) olive oil
- 200 g (8 oz) peeled tomatoes
- 1 dl (3 fl oz) white wine
- a pinch of salt and pepper
- white flour
- a sprig of parsley, finely chopped
- water
- 2 garlic cloves

In a frying pan, brown the garlic and the floured fish steaks in the oil.
Add the wine, the peeled tomatoes and a little water. Add salt, pepper, cover the pan and cook for about 10 minutes.
Serve hot sprinkled with finely chopped parsley.

Variation: using the same ingredients, you can prepare dusky sea perch, yellowtail and any kind of fish used for making soup (red bandfish, weevers, congers, etc.).

Smothered swordfish
Pisci spata a l'agghiotta

- 4 swordfish steaks weighing 200 g (8 oz) each
- 1 onion, finely chopped
- 2 sachets of saffron
- 2 dl (6 fl oz) olive oil
- 2 dl (6 fl oz) white wine
- a pinch of salt and pepper
- a sprig of parsley, finely chopped
- white flour
- water

In a frying pan, brown the chopped onion in the oil.
As soon as it starts to become golden brown, add the floured fish steaks, and fry on both sides. Add the wine and the saffron dissolved in water.
Add salt, pepper and cook for about 10 minutes over a moderate heat. Serve the fish piping hot sprinkled with chopped parsley.

Variation: with the same ingredients you can cook any kind of fish steaks (dusky sea perch, cod, salt cod, etc.) and any kind of fish used for soups (stargazer, gurnards, weevers, red bandfish etc.).

Messina-style swordfish
Pisci spata a missinisi

- 4 swordfish steaks weighing 200 g (8 oz) each
- 1 dl (3 fl oz) dry white wine
- 2 dl (6 fl oz) olive oil
- 200 g (8 oz) peeled tomatoes
- 100 g (4 oz) pitted green olives
- 50 g (2 oz) desalted capers
- 3 potatoes, thinly sliced
- a pinch of salt and pepper
- white flour
- a sprig of parsley, finely chopped
- water

In a frying pan, brown the floured fish steaks on both sides in the oil. Add a few dashes of wine, the pitted olives, the desalted capers, the peeled tomatoes and dilute the sauce with a little water. Add salt, pepper and arrange the potatoes over the fish. Cover the pan and cook over a moderate heat for about 15 minutes. Arrange the fish steaks on a serving dish and cover with the sauce. Sprinkle with chopped parsley and serve piping hot.

Variations: use the same method for any kind of fish steaks: dusky sea perch, yellowtail, albacore, cod, salt cod etc.

Palermo-style swordfish
Pisci spata a palermitana

- 4 swordfish steaks weighing 200 g (8 oz) each
- 3 garlic cloves, finely chopped
- breadcrumbs
- 2 dl (6 fl oz) olive oil
- a pinch of salt and pepper
- a pinch of oregano

In a bowl, mix the breadcrumbs, garlic, salt, pepper and oregano. Brush the fish steaks with oil and coat with the breadcrumb mixture. Arrange on a red-hot, oiled grill and cook on both sides for about 10 minutes. Serve hot with a little oil.

Variations: use the same ingredients for other fish steaks such as dusky sea perch, yellowtail, albacore, etc.

Octopus in tomato sauce
Purpiteddi murati

- 10 octopuses weighing 100 g (4 oz) each
- 4 ripe tomatoes
- 1 onion
- 2 dl (6 fl oz) olive oil
- a pinch of salt and pepper
- a sprig of parsley

Clean the octopuses, empty the heads and remove the mouth. In an earthenware pot, brown the onion in the oil. Add the diced tomatoes, and, if desired, an ink sack. Add the octopuses, cover the pot and cook over a moderate heat for about 20 minutes. Uncover, place the octopuses in a bowl, reduce the sauce and then pour over the octopuses. They can be served either hot or cold, covered with chopped parsley.

Fried baby sardine fishcakes
Purpetti di 'nunnata fritti

- 800 g (32 oz) baby sardines
- 100 g (4 oz) grated parmesan cheese
- a pinch of salt
- a sprig of parsley
- strong flour
- 1 egg
- olive oil

In a bowl, mix the baby sardines with the flour, parmesan cheese, salt, parsley and egg until well blended. Heat the oil in a frying pan and add the mixture one spoonful at a time. Fry each side for about five minutes. Place on kitchen paper to remove any excess oil and serve hot.

Grilled baby sardine fishcakes
Purpetti di 'nunnata di sardi arrustuti

- 800 g (32 oz) baby sardines
- white flour
- olive oil
- a pinch of salt and pepper
- a sprig of parsley, finely chopped
- 1 lemon

In a bowl, mix the baby sardines, with the flour, salt, pepper, parsley and a little oil until well blended. Oil the grill. Put the slightly flattened fishcakes on top. Cook them over a moderate heat on both sides for 12 minutes or so. Serve hot with a drizzle of oil and lemon wedges on the side.

Catanese-style sardines
Sardi a linguati a catanisi

- 600 g (1 24 oz) boned sardines
- 120 g (5 oz) breadcrumbs
- 50 g (2 oz) grated caciocavallo cheese
- 3 eggs
- white flour

- 2 tbsp desalted capers
- 4 dl (12 fl oz) vinegar
- olive oil
- a pinch of salt and pepper
- a spring of parsley, finely chopped

Clean the sardines and marinate them in the vinegar. Put 50 g (2 oz) of breadcrumbs, finely chopped capers, salt, pepper, parsley, and cheese into a bowl and mix together with one egg. Drain the sardines and lay them flat onto a work surface. Put some of the prepared mixture on one side of the sardines and close them up. Dust with flour, dip in beaten egg, coat with breadcrumbs and fry in hot oil. Serve hot.

Marinated sardines
Sardi a linguati

- 1 kg (2 lbs) fresh boned sardines
- 8 garlic cloves
- 3 dl (9 fl oz) olive oil
- 3 dl (9 fl oz) white wine vinegar
- a pinch of salt
- a small sprig of fresh mint

In a bowl, prepare the marinade by beating together the oil, the vinegar, the sliced garlic, salt and mint leaves.
Put a layer of sardines in a glass dish and cover with the marinade.
Keep adding layers of sardines, alternating with the marinade until you have used up all the ingredients.
Put in the fridge and leave to rest for 24 hours before serving.

*photo

Stuffed sardines
Sardi a "beccaficu"

- 40 fresh sardines
- 1 loaf of sliced sandwich bread
- 50 g (2 oz) raisins and pine nuts
- 30 g (1 oz) anchovies
- 1 dl (3 fl oz) vinegar
- 50 g (2 oz) sugar
- a pinch of salt
- 1 dl (3 fl oz) orange juice
- 1 dl (3 fl oz) lemon juice
- 2 dl (6 fl oz) olive oil
- 50 bay leaves

Clean the sardines and open them up flat. In a bowl, soak the raisins and the pine nuts in vinegar and sugar for about 5 minutes. Add the crumbled bread, the salt, the anchovies, the orange and lemon juice and a little oil. Mix all together until the mixture is soft and compact. Line up the sardines on a work surface and put a little of the mixture in the middle of each one. Carefully roll them up making sure that the tails are on the outside. Lay them side by side in an ovenproof dish, with the tails facing upwards and a bay leaf between each one. Drizzle a little oil over them and bake in a pre-heated 180°C (350°F) oven for 5 minutes. Serve warm or cold.

Scorpion fish in red sauce
Scrofano a brodiceddu

- 8 scorpion fish weighing 200 g (8 oz) each
- 4 garlic cloves
- 2 dl (6 fl oz) olive oil
- 2 dl (6 fl oz) dry white wine
- 200 g (8 oz) peeled tomatoes
- a pinch of salt and pepper
- a sprig of parsley, finely chopped
- white flour

Clean the scorpion fish and dust with flour. Heat the oil in a saucepan and brown the fish for a few minutes over a low heat. Add the sliced garlic, pour over the wine and add the diced peeled tomatoes. Correct the salt and add a little pepper. Add the chopped parsley and dilute the cooking liquid with a little water. Cook over a moderate heat for about 12 minutes or so.

Grilled cuttlefish
Sicci arrustuti

- 4 cuttlefish weighing 300 g (12 oz) each
- 2 dl (6 fl oz) olive oil
- a pinch of salt
- a sprig of parsley, finely chopped

Clean the cuttlefish, removing the bone and the mouth. Brush with oil, sprinkle with a little salt then place on a red-hot grill. Cook on both sides over a low heat for about 10 minutes. Serve hot with a little olive oil and chopped parsley.

Grilled mackerel
Scurmi arrustuti

- 8 mackerel weighing 200 g (8 oz) each
- 2 dl (6 fl oz) olive oil
- a pinch of salt and pepper

- juice of 1/2 lemon
- a pinch of oregano

Clean the mackerel, gut and remove the gills. Brush them with oil and sprinkle with a little salt. Grill them on both sides over a moderate heat for about 10 minutes. Serve hot with a sauce made from oil, lemon, oregano and pepper.

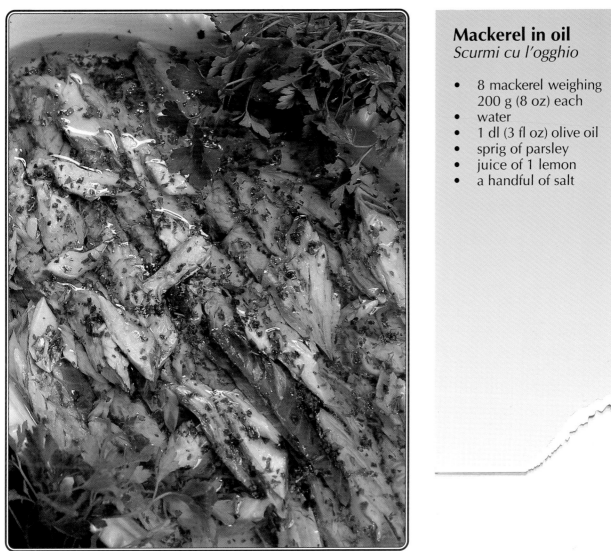

Mackerel in oil
Scurmi cu l'ogghio

- 8 mackerel weighing 200 g (8 oz) each
- water
- 1 dl (3 fl oz) olive oil
- sprig of parsley
- juice of 1 lemon
- a handful of salt

Clean the mackerel, gut them and remove the gills. Put them into a saucepan and cover with cold water. Add a handful of salt. Cook them over a moderate heat for about 10 minutes. Leave to cool, remove the bones and lay them in rows on a serving dish. Add olive oil, lemon juice, salt and chopped parsley.

Grilled sole
Linguati arrustuti

- 8 soles weighing 200 g (8 oz) each
- 1 dl (3 fl oz) olive oil
- a pinch of salt
- a sprig of parsley, finely chopped

Wash and drain the soles, then brush with oil. Sprinkle with salt and arrange on a pre-heated grill. Cook on both sides for about 10 minutes.
Serve with oil and garnish with finely chopped parsley.

Fried scabbardfish
"Spatula" fritta

- 4 scabbardfish steaks weighing 200 g (8 oz) each
- strong flour
- olive oil
- a pinch of salt

Dust the fish steaks with flour, then put them into a frying pan with sizzling oil. Fry them for a few minutes. Serve hot, sprinkled with salt.

Little cuttlefish kebabs

- 40 little cuttlefish
- 2 dl (6 fl oz) olive oil
- a pinch of salt
- a sprig of parsley, finely chopped

Clean the cuttlefish, removing the bone and thread onto wooden skewers. Brush with oil, add a little salt and arrange on a grill. Cook over a low heat for about 5 minutes. Drizzle with oil, sprinkle with parsley and serve hot.

Messina-style prawn kebabs
Spitini di gammareddi a missinisi

- 600 g (24 oz) peeled prawns
- 1 garlic clove (optional)
- 80 g (3 oz) breadcrumbs
- 30 g (1 oz) grated caciocavallo cheese
- juice of 1 lemon
- 1 dl (3 fl oz) olive oil
- a pinch of salt and pepper
- a sprig of parsley, finely chopped

Thread the prawns onto short wooden or metal skewers. In a bowl, mix the breadcrumbs, cheese, salt, pepper and parsley. In a shallow dish, pour the oil, the lemon juice and add the garlic. Dip the kebabs in the oil, drain and then coat with the breadcrumb mixture. Brush the griddle with oil and when it is red-hot, position the kebabs. Cook on both sides for a few minutes and serve piping hot.

Swordfish kebabs with citron
Spitini di pisci spata

- 20 chunks of swordfish flesh, weighing 30 g (1 oz) each and approx. 2 cm (1 inch) thick
- 24 citron leaves
- 100 g (4 oz) margarine
- 1 dl (3 fl oz) olive oil
- 150 g (6 oz) butter
- juice of 5 citrons
- 50 g (2 oz) desalted capers, finely chopped
- a pinch of salt

Prepare the kebabs by threading the swordfish chunks alternated with the citron leaves onto skewers. Brown in a frying pan with the oil and margarine. When they are almost cooked, remove the fat and replace with the butter and citron juice.
Add the capers, salt, and pepper and continue cooking over a low heat until the butter melts. Serve the kebabs hot with the cooking juice.

Tuna with onion sauce
Tunnina cu a cipuddata

- 4 tuna steaks, weighing 200 g (8 oz) each
- 4 onions
- 3 dl (9 fl oz) olive oil
- a pinch of salt
- a sprig of parsley, finely chopped
- water
- white flour
- 100 g (4 oz) sugar
- 2 dl (6 fl oz) wine vinegar

Flour the tuna and fry for about 5 minutes. Arrange the fish on a serving dish. In another frying pan, soften the sliced onion in the water. As soon as it becomes soft and transparent, add the oil and let it brown. Add the sugar and when it starts to caramelise, add the vinegar and salt. Cook for a few more minutes then pour over the fish. Serve warm or cold garnished with chopped parsley.

Baked tuna
Tunnina 'nfurnata

- 1 kg (2 lbs) tuna in one piece
- 1 dl (3 fl oz) olive oil
- a pinch of salt
- a pinch of chilli powder
- fresh rosemary

In a baking dish, pour enough oil to cover the bottom. Arrange the tuna, add salt, chilli and the rosemary. Bake for an hour at about 150°C (300°F), turning occasionally so that it browns evenly. If necessary, add a little water to prevent the fish from drying out. Slice and serve hot with a few spoonfuls of the cooking juice.

Variation: the tuna cooked in such a way can be served cold with a herb and garlic sauce, or a dressing made with oil, lemon juice and parsley, or with diluted sweet and sour onion sauce.

Fried tuna
Tunnina fritta

- 4 tuna steaks, weighing 200 g (8 oz) each
- olive oil
- strong flour
- a pinch of salt and pepper

Heat the oil in a frying pan and dust the fish steaks with flour. Fry them over a moderate heat for 8 minutes on both sides.

Add salt, pepper and serve piping hot.

Tuna with tomato sauce
Tunnina 'mbuttunata a ragù

- 1 kg (2 lbs) fresh tuna (in one piece)
- 5 garlic cloves
- 3 dl (9 fl oz) olive oil
- a handful of salt
- a pinch of pepper
- plenty of fresh mint leaves
- 200 g (8 oz) tomato puree
- water
- 1 onion

In a deep saucepan, brown the onion in the oil. Add the diluted tomato puree, salt, pepper, sprinkle with mint leaves and cook for about 10 minutes. Make a few cuts in the tuna with a knife and fill with garlic, salt, pepper and some mint leaves.

Brown the tuna in a frying pan with a little oil until golden all over. Add to the sauce and cook for about an hour. Serve warm with the sauce.

Baked tuna fish with an onion and anchovy sauce
Tunnina a sfinciuni

- 4 tuna steaks, weighing 200 g (8 oz) each
- 3 onions
- 100 g (4 oz) anchovies
- 200 g (8 oz) tomato puree
- 3 dl (9 fl oz) olive oil
- 100 g (4 oz) breadcrumbs
- a pinch of salt and pepper
- water

In a frying pan, brown the tuna steaks in a little of the oil on both sides, and then arrange in a baking dish. In another pan, brown the chopped onion in the rest of the oil and add the anchovies. Mash them so that they dissolve completely. Add the tomato puree diluted in the water, add salt, pepper and cook for 10 minutes until the sauce thickens. Pour the sauce over the tuna steaks, cover with breadcrumbs and bake for about 5 minutes at 180°C (350°F).

Grilled goatfish
Trigghi arrustuti

- 8 goatfish, weighing 200 g (8 oz) each
- 2 dl (6 fl oz) olive oil
- a pinch of salt
- a sprig of parsley, finely chopped

Clean the fish thoroughly and brush with oil. Add a little salt and put them on a red-hot griddle. Cook on both sides for about 10 minutes. Serve hot with a drizzle of oil and finely chopped parsley.

Goatfish baked in foil
Trigghi in tianu

- 8 goatfish, weighing 150 g (6 oz) each
- 150 g (6 oz) squid rings
- 100 g (4 oz) peeled prawns
- 300 g (12 oz) mussels
- 4 garlic cloves
- 3 dl (9 fl oz) olive oil
- 2 dl (6 fl oz) white wine
- 200 g (8 oz) peeled tomatoes
- a pinch of salt and pepper
- a sprig of parsley, finely chopped
- water
- white flour

Clean and gut the fish, removing the gills and scales. Dust with flour and fry in a shallow saucepan in the oil and garlic. Add the squid, prawns and mussels and simmer for about 3 minutes. Pour in the wine and add the tomatoes. Add salt and pepper and dilute the sauce with a little water. Cover the pan and cook over a moderate heat for about 12 minutes. Serve with finely chopped parsley.

Fried goatfish
Trigghi fritti

- 8 goatfish, weighing 150 g (6 oz) each
- strong flour
- olive oil
- a pinch of salt

Clean the fish, dust with flour and fry in hot oil. Cook slowly on both sides for about 10 minutes. Serve hot, with a pinch of salt.

Saffron goatfish
Trigghi c'a zafarana

- 8 goatfish, weighing 200 g (8 oz) each
- 2 sachets of saffron
- 2 dl (6 fl oz) olive oil
- 2 dl (6 fl oz) dry white wine
- water
- white flour
- a pinch of salt
- 1 onion

Dust the cleaned, drained fish with flour. Heat the oil in a shallow frying pan and add the fish, browning on both sides for about 3 minutes.
Add the chopped onion, saffron and wine, diluting the sauce with a little water. Correct the salt and cook for about 5 minutes.

Fish soup
Suppa di pisci

- 1 kg fish for soup (gurnard, scorpion fish, John dory, brill etc.)
- 200 g (8 oz) squid
- 150 g (6 oz) peeled prawns
- 500 g (1 lb) mussels
- 2 dl (6 fl oz) olive oil
- 4 garlic cloves
- 2 dl (6 fl oz) white wine
- 300 g (12 oz) peeled tomatoes
- a pinch of salt and pepper
- a sprig of parsley, finely chopped
- white flour
- water

Clean the fish and cut into chunks. Cut the squid in rings. In a pot, preferably earthenware, heat the oil, and then add the tomatoes, the fish, the molluscs (squids and mussels), the shellfish (prawns) and garlic. Cook for a few minutes. Pour in the wine, add salt, pepper and cook covered for a further 10 minutes. Add a little water to dilute the sauce. Add finely chopped parsley and serve hot.

Aniseed biscuits
Viscotta all'anici

- 1 kg (2 lbs) flour
- 800 g (32 oz) sugar
- 1 tsp aniseed
- 700 g (28 oz) eggs weighed in their shells
- a pinch of vanilla and powdered ammonia
- butter

Whip the egg whites in a bowl until stiff. Add the flour mixed with the sugar, vanilla, ammonia and aniseed and mix until well blended. Add the egg yolks. Knead thoroughly until you get a soft, well-blended mixture. Form half-moon shapes (about 3 cm (1 inch) thick). Arrange on a greased baking tin and bake in a moderate oven for about 15 minutes.

* photo

Blancmange
Biancu manciari

- 1 l (32 fl oz) milk
- 200 g (8 oz) sugar
- 100 g (4 oz) starch
- 2 g (0.10 oz) vanilla

In a saucepan, mix the sugar and starch with a wooden spoon. Add the milk a little at a time, making sure that no lumps form.
Place the pan over the heat, add the vanilla, and stir until the cream looks velvety and thick. Remove from the heat, pour into bowls and leave to cool.

Variation: use the zest of an orange or lemon or cocoa instead of the vanilla.

Sesame biscuits
Viscotta riggina

- 1 kg (2 lbs) flour
- 400 g (16 oz) sugar
- 400 g (16 oz) butter
- 2 dl (6 fl oz) milk
- a pinch of vanilla
- a few drops of orange essence
- 4 eggs
- sesame seeds
- a pinch of ammonia

Mix the sugar, the essence, the ammonia, the butter and the eggs into a bowl. Add the flour and knead until it is of a good consistency. Leave to rest in a hot place for about an hour. Form sticks of about 5 cm (2 inches), dip in a bowl with milk and then coat with sesame seeds. Arrange on a greased baking tray and bake in a moderate oven for about 15 minutes.

St Martin's biscuits
Viscotta di San Martinu

- 1 kg (2 lbs) flour
- 270 g (11 oz) sugar
- 200 g (8 oz) butter
- 50 g (2 oz) yeast
- 40 g (2 oz) aniseed
- 10 g (1/2 oz) cinnamon
- 3 dl (9 fl oz) warm water

On a working surface, mix the flour, sugar, cinnamon and aniseed together. Make a hollow in the middle and add the butter and the yeast.

Knead well, add warm water a little at a time until you get a soft paste. Roll the mixture into little round shapes about 5 cm (2 inches) in diameter and then arrange on a greased baking tray. Leave them to rise in a warm place for about an hour. Bake in a moderate oven until they are golden brown.

They should be eaten with a dry Marsala wine or, if preferred, Passito or muscatel wines.

Fruit ring
Cucciddatu

- 500 g (1 lb) flour
- 200 g (8 oz) sugar
- 300 g (10 oz) butter
- 4 eggs
- 1 dl (3 fl oz) milk
- 300 g (10 oz) dried figs
- 60 g (2 oz) pistachios
- 150 g (6 oz) walnut kernels
- 50 g (2 oz) plain chocolate flakes
- 100 g (4 oz) sultana raisins
- 150 g (6 oz) toasted almonds, finely chopped
- 5 ground cloves
- 250 g (10 oz) diced candied pumpkin
- a pinch of cinnamon
- marmalade
- 1/2 glass of Marsala

Knead the flour, butter, sugar, three eggs, a little salt and the milk on the work surface, forming a smooth dough. Cover with a cloth and leave to rest for about 2 hours.

Put the chopped figs, 1 egg, the walnuts, almonds, raisins, cloves, cinnamon and half a glass of Marsala in a saucepan. Cook for about 10 minutes. Remove from the heat, add 3 tablespoons of marmalade, and leave to cool.

Roll out the dough into an approx. 1 cm (0.5 inch) thick long, rectangle shape. Put the filling in the middle and fold the two sides of the rectangle then roll forming a long tube. Join the two ends together to make a ring; arrange on a greased baking tin and make a few cuts along the dough deep enough for the filling to show through.

Bake in a hot oven for about 30 minutes. Remove from the oven and brush the dough ring with a tablespoon of marmalade dissolved in water. Sprinkle with chopped pistachios and bake for another 5 minutes. Decorate with candied peel and leave to cool before removing from the baking tray.

Cannoli
Cannola

- 800 g (32 oz) flour
- 150 g (6 oz) lard
- oil
- 4 eggs
- 1 dl (3 fl oz) muscatel or white wine
- 75 g (3 oz) sugar
- a pinch of salt
- a pinch of vanilla
- ricotta cream
- candied orange peel or cherries

Put the flour onto a work surface, making a hollow in the middle and place the lard, sugar, white or muscatel wine and the eggs. Mix together, kneading well until a firm dough forms. Leave to rest for about 1 hour. Roll out so that it is quite thin and cut out circles of about 10 cm (4 inches) in diameter. These circles are to be rolled around 12 cm (5-inch) long tubes (tin or reed), which have been greased with oil. In a large, deep saucepan, deep fry the snaps until they are golden. Leave to cool. Remove the snaps from the tubes. Fill with ricotta cream (see recipe), dust with icing sugar and garnish with candied orange peel or cherries.

Variation: coat the inside of the snaps with melted chocolate so that the ricotta does not make them too soggy.

Baked *cassata* pie
Cassata infornata

- short-crust pastry
- icing sugar
- ricotta cream
- butter

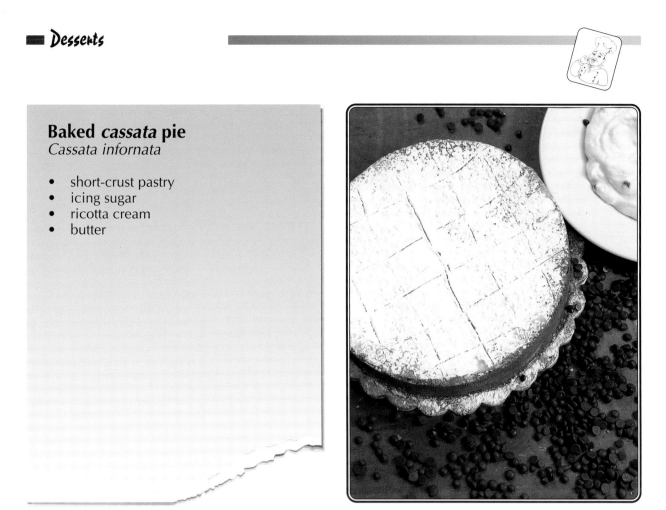

Divide the short-crust pastry (see recipe) into two parts. Form two disks, leaving them quite thick. Grease and flour a baking tin and line with one half of the pastry (bottom and sides). Fill with the ricotta cream (see recipe) and cover with the remaining pastry. Prick the top with a fork and bake for about 30 minutes. Leave to cool, turn out onto a plate and dust with icing sugar.

Variation: melon gel may be used in place of ricotta cream.

Sicilian *cassata* cake
Cassata siciliana

- sponge cake
- ricotta cream
- marzipan
- 150 g (6 oz) icing sugar
- water
- candied fruit: mandarins, pears, oranges, plums, cherries and candied pumpkin

Prepare the sponge cake, the ricotta cream and the marzipan following the recipes found in this book.

For the icing, melt the icing sugar with a ladle of water over a low heat until the sugar starts to go stringy. Make sure the mixture stays brilliant white.

Dust a baking tin with slightly flared edges with icing sugar and line the edge with strips of marzipan and sponge cake. Cover the bottom with strips of sponge cake laid side by side. Fill with ricotta cream, spreading with a spatula. Add pieces of sponge cake to the mixture. Leave the cassata to rest for about an hour, then turn it out onto a plate. Pour the warm icing over the cake, spreading it out with a spatula and leave to cool.

Decorate with the candied fruit, putting the mandarin in the middle. Put slices of candies pumpkin or citron around the edge. Use the other fruit to make a colourful pattern.

Pastry cream

- 1 l (32 fl oz) milk
- 300 g (10 oz) sugar
- 150 g (6 oz) flour
- 8 egg yolks
- a pinch of vanilla
- 1 tsp grated lemon zest

Boil the milk together with the lemon zest and a pinch of vanilla. In a saucepan, beat the eggs together with the sugar and the flour. Pour the warm milk over the egg yolks a little at a time stirring continuously so that no lumps form. Reduce the cream over a moderate heat for 3 to 4 minutes, stirring all the time. When ready, remove from heat, pour into a bowl and leave to cool.

Suggestion: this cream can be used to fill cream puffs, cakes, pies and many other kinds of desserts.

Ricotta cream

- 300 g (12 oz) ricotta cheese
- 150 g (6 oz) sugar
- a pinch of vanilla
- a tbsp plain chocolate drops

In a bowl, blend the ricotta, together with the sugar and vanilla, and leave to rest for about 12 hours. Mix well and sieve at least twice so as to make the cream smoother. Add the chocolate drops and mix one more time.

Orange tart

- 500 g (1 lb) short-crust pastry
- custard
- 5 oranges
- 5 small candied cherries
- fruit jelly

Line a greased, floured baking tin with the short-crust pastry. Cover with greaseproof paper and bake in a hot oven for about 20 minutes. When almost cooked, remove the paper and bake for another 5 minutes. Remove from the oven and leave to cool.
Fill with the custard, and put back in the oven for another 5 minutes.
Decorate with slices of orange and red cherries. Cover with the jelly and leave to cool before serving.

photo

Wheat pudding
Cuccìa

- 1 kg (2 lbs) soft wheat
- 900 g (36 oz) ricotta cream
- 25 g (1 oz) finely chopped pistachios
- 25 g (1 oz) small candied cherries
- a pinch of salt
- a pinch of cinnamon
- 10 g (1/2 oz) cocoa powder
- water

Soak the wheat for 24 hours in cold water, changing the water regularly. Boil some salted water and pour in the wheat, which should be simmered for at least 5 hours over a low heat. Once cooked, drain and leave to cool. Mix carefully with the ricotta cream (see recipe).
Add a sprinkle of cocoa and cinnamon and decorate with the pistachios and cherries.

Variation: use blancmange instead of ricotta cream.

St Joseph's cream puffs

- 350 g (14 oz) soft flour
- 5 eggs
- 100 g (4 oz) butter
- 4 dl (12 fl oz) water
- a pinch of salt
- candied orange peel and red cherries
- ricotta cream
- lard

Put the water, butter and salt into a pan and bring to the boil.

Add the flour and mix with a wooden spoon for about 10 minutes until the mixture becomes soft and compact. Remove from the heat and turn out onto a plate. Roll it out to let it cool down.

Add the egg yolks and knead the mixture.

Beat the egg whites until stiff and fold in the mixture.

The mixture should be soft and creamy. Drop spoonfuls of the mixture into a deep frying pan full of lard so they form fritters. Let them cool and cut a slit in them with a knife. Prepare the ricotta cream.

Spread the cream over the fritters. Decorate with the orange peel and red cherries.

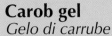

Carob gel
Gelo di carrube

- 10 ripe carobs
- 90 g (3 oz) starch for every l (32 fl oz) of juice
- 200 g (8 oz) sugar

After having broken the carobs into little pieces, place them in a container, cover with water and leave to soak for 2 days. Then boil them in the same water for 30 minutes over a low heat. Leave to cool and filter the juice. Separate the juice into four equal parts. Boil three parts with the sugar. Dissolve the starch in the fourth part and add it to the boiling juice. Mix with a wooden spoon until it is thick. Pour into glass bowls and when the mixture is cool, place in the fridge.

Watermelon gel
Gelo di muluni

- 1 l (32 fl oz) water-melon juice
- 80 g (3 oz) starch for every l (32 fl oz) of juice
- 150 g (6 oz) sugar
- 4 drops of jasmine essence
- 3 drops of cinnamon essence
- chopped pistachios
- plain chocolate flakes or drops

Remove the skin and black seeds from the watermelon and sieve. Divide the juice in four parts. Dissolve the starch in one part of the juice. Put the other three parts on the heat along with the sugar, and as soon as it starts to boil, add the dissolved starch. Add the jasmine and cinnamon essences. Continue cooking, stirring continuously with a wooden spoon, until it starts to thicken. Pour into individual bowls and leave to cool for about two hours. Decorate with the chocolate, pistachios and some jasmine flowers. Put in the fridge for a few hours and serve cold.

Spicy biscuits
Mustazzoli

- 500 g (1 lb) flour
- 500 g (1 lb) sugar
- 4 drops of clove essence
- a pinch of cinnamon
- 2 dl (6 fl oz) warm water
- butter

On a work surface, knead the flour with the sugar, clove essence and warm water to form a smooth dough. Roll it out to a thickness of about 2-3 cm (1 inch).
Cut the pastry into irregular 4 cm (1.5 inches) shapes. Arrange on a greased baking tray and bake in a moderate oven for about 40 minutes.

* photo

Sponge cake

- 10 eggs
- 300 g (12 oz) sugar
- 250 g (10 oz) soft flour
- a pinch of vanilla
- butter

Whisk the egg yolks thoroughly with the sugar until the mixture turns foamy. Add the flour and vanilla a little at a time and mix carefully. Beat the egg whites until stiff and fold in the mixture. Pour into a greased and floured cake tin of about 30 cm (15 inches) in diameter and bake in a moderate oven for about 40 minutes.

Sponge cake is an excellent base for lots of desserts, from *cassata* to *zuppa inglese* (a kind of trifle). It can actually be covered with all kinds of cream.

Choux pastry

- 600 g (24 oz) flour
- 200 g (8 oz) butter
- 1 l (32 fl oz) water
- 16 eggs

Heat the water in a pan and add the flour and butter as soon as it starts to boil, stirring with a wooden spoon. Cook over a moderate heat for about 5 minutes. The result is a thick pastry which you should then allow to cool.
Put the pastry into a bowl, add the eggs one at a time. Work the pastry until it becomes smooth and soft. Leave to rest for about 2 hours. Grease a baking tray and evenly space out spoonfuls of the pastry. Put the tray in the oven and when the buns have risen and turned golden brown in colour, remove from the oven and leave to cool.

Variation: fill the choux buns with orange, lemon or mandarin-flavoured custard or ricotta cream, etc.

Short-crust pastry

- 1 kg (2 lbs) flour
- 400 g (16 oz) softened butter
- 400 g (16 oz) sugar
- 6 eggs
- 1 tsp grated orange and lemon zest

Put the flour on a work surface and make a hollow in the middle for the softened butter, the sugar, the eggs and the grated zest. Knead the ingredients until they form a smooth dough. Place the pastry in a bowl and cover with a towel. Leave to rest for a few minutes and finally put in the fridge for about an hour.

Variation: short-crust pastry may be also used to make biscuits which are then dusted with icing sugar.

Almond paste

- 500 g (1 lb) almonds
- 500 g (1 lb) icing sugar
- 50 g (2 oz) butter
- 2 eggs or 4 egg yolks
- 5 drops of almond essence

In a pan, boil 1/2 l (18 fl oz) of water. Turn off the heat and add the almonds, leaving them to soak for 10 minutes. Drain, peel, dry and finely chop them mixed with the sugar. Add the eggs and the essence, and continue mixing until a smooth paste forms. If it is not to be used immediately, keep the paste in the fridge.

Variation: almond paste may be used to make all kinds of biscuits, decorated with pine nuts, candied peel or cherries, and it can also be used to make little balls, filled with fruit jams (citron jam, marmalade etc.) and then baked for about 15 minutes.

Marzipan
Pasta riali

- 100 g (4 oz) almond flour
- 200 g (8 oz) sugar
- 3 drops of almond essence
- a pinch of vanilla
- 1 tsp of honey
- a few drops of food colouring (green)

Mix the almond flour with the sugar, almond essence, a pinch of vanilla, honey and food colouring dissolved in a little bit of water.
Mix together carefully to form a soft mixture.

Variation: this mixture can be piped into stoned dates or used to sandwich the two halves of a candied cherry or two walnut kernels together. Sprinkle the latter with caster sugar.

Immaculate fritters

- 700 g (28 oz) flour
- 6 dl (9 fl oz) milk
- 40 g (2 oz) yeast
- 6 eggs
- 10 g (0.5 oz) sugar
- 3 g (0.10 oz) salt

For the decoration:
- sugar

In a bowl, dissolve the flour in 4 dl (12 fl oz) of milk. Add the eggs, the salt and the sugar and mix thoroughly. Separately, heat up the milk and when warm, add to the yeast so that it dissolves. Add to the mixture, cover and make it rise for about 45 minutes. Pour spoonfuls of the mixture in hot oil and let them brown. Place on kitchen paper to remove the excess oil. Coat the fritters with the sugar and serve hot or cold.

Honey and fruit sticks
Petrafennula

- 700 g (28 oz) natural honey
- 300 g (12 oz) orange peel
- 150 g (6 oz) lemon or citron peel
- 5 g (0.30 oz) vanilla
- 5 g (0.30 oz) cinnamon

Put the honey, orange and lemon peel into a pan; cook over a very low heat until the mixture takes on a hard consistency.
Add the cinnamon and vanilla. Pour into oiled cylindrical tins of about 10 cm (4 inches) long. Leave to cool, turn out and wrap in small pieces of greaseproof paper.

* photo

Messina-style fried pastry pyramid
Pignulata a missinisi

- 1 kg (2 lbs) flour
- 400 g (16 oz) sugar
- 400 g (16 oz) cocoa
- 12 egg yolks
- oil or lard
- water

Knead the flour with the egg yolks and half of the sugar until it is smooth and thick. Shape into tubes, cut them into 1-2 cm (0.5 inch) pieces and fry them in boiling oil or lard for about 2 minutes. Dry on kitchen paper and pile up on a plate to form a pyramid. Prepare the icing by dissolving the remaining sugar and cocoa in a little bit of water over a moderate heat. Pour it over the pyramid and leave to cool.

Variation: make two pyramids, pouring the cocoa icing over one (using half the amount of sugar and cocoa) and pouring ordinary white sugar icing flavoured with lemon zest over the other.

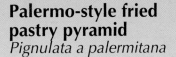

Palermo-style fried pastry pyramid
Pignulata a palermitana

- 500 g (1 lb) flour
- 200 g (8 oz) sugar
- 150 g (6 oz) honey
- 6 egg yolks
- oil or lard
- water

Knead the flour with the eggs and half the sugar until it is smooth. Shape into tubes, cut them into 1-2 cm (0.5 inch) pieces and then fry in boiling oil or lard for about 2 minutes. In a separate saucepan, melt the rest of the sugar with the honey over a moderate heat. Add the fried pastry pieces and continue cooking. As soon as they start sticking together, turn them out onto an oiled marble board making little piles and then leave to cool.

Lent cakes

- 800 g (32 oz) almonds
- 1.200 g (48 oz) flour
- 1.050 g (42 oz) sugar
- 10 eggs
- 10 g (0.5 oz) ammonia
- a pinch of vanilla
- a pinch of cinnamon
- a few drops of yellow food colouring
- butter

On a work surface, knead the flour with the whole almonds, sugar, eggs, ammonia, vanilla, cinnamon and yellow food colouring until it is smooth and thick. Place the mixture into buttered 20 cm x 10 cm (8 x 4 inch) baking tins. Bake for about 15 minutes. When the Lent cakes are cooked, turn them out and cut into 3-4 cm (1 inch) slices.

Iced biscuits
Taralli

- 1 kg (2 lbs) flour
- 1 kg (2 lbs) sugar
- 12 eggs
- 2 dl (6 fl oz) lukewarm water
- zest of 1 lemon
- 1 little glass of anisetta
- 1 small sachet of vanilla
- butter
- sugar icing

Mix the flour with the sugar, egg yolks, anisetta and water. Beat the egg whites until stiff and fold in the mixture. Knead until soft and consistent. Cut into little pieces big enough to make 10 cm (4 inch) long rolls, then set aside for a few hours. Grease a baking tray with butter, place the dough and form rings. Bake in the oven for about half an hour. When almost cooked, remove from the oven and coat with warm icing sugar flavoured with lemon zest and vanilla. Bake for a few more minutes in the hot oven. Leave to cool and serve.

Fried pastry with cream
Testa di turcu

For the pastry:
- 200 g (8 oz) flour
- 4 tbsp sugar
- 2 eggs
- oil

For the pastry cream:
- 1 l (32 fl oz) milk
- 1 stick of cinnamon
- zest of 1 lemon
- 70 g (3 oz) starch

For the decoration:
- plain chocolate drops
- ground cinnamon
- little coloured sugar balls

Put the flour and a pinch of sugar into a bowl and mix with the eggs until well blended. Roll out the pastry, cut it into thin strips and deep fry in boiling oil.

Boil three quarters of the milk with the sugar, cinnamon stick and the lemon zest. In another bowl dissolve the starch in the left over milk and add to the boiling milk. Cook until it forms a very thick cream.

On a serving dish, alternate a layer of custard with a layer of pastry, finishing with a final layer of custard. Put it in the fridge for about 2 hours.

Sprinkle the top with ground cinnamon, decorate with coloured sugar balls and chocolate drops. Serve cold.

Triumph of gluttony
Triunfu di gula

- 2 layers of sponge cake
- 800 g (32 oz) of your favourite jam
- 400 g (16 oz) marzipan
- 800 g (32 oz) ricotta cheese
- 800 g (32 oz) pastry cream
- 500 g (1 lb) pistachios, finely chopped
- 300 g (12 oz) fruit jelly
- 300 g (12 oz) mixed candied fruit

Put one of the layers of sponge cake onto a serving dish and cover it with jam. Then put a similar sized layer of marzipan on top and spread with custard and ricotta cream. Cover with the second layer of sponge cake and coat the sides with the finely chopped pistachios. Cover the top with the fruit jelly and decorate with candied fruit.

SUMMARY

PASTA AND LENTIL SOUP, 55
PASTA TIMBALE WITH SARDINES, 75
PASTA WITH AUBERGINES AND TOMATO SAUCE, 64
PASTA WITH CAULIFLOWER, 59
PASTA WITH DRIED BROAD BEANS, 61
PASTA WITH FRESH RICOTTA CHEESE, 68
PASTA WITH FRIED COURGETTES, 73
PASTA WITH PEAS, 66
PASTA WITH PEELED TOMATOES, 66
PASTA WITH PORK MEAT SAUCE, 67
PASTA WITH PRAWNS, 62
PASTA WITH RED ANCHOVIES, 57
PASTA WITH RED TUNA, 70

PASTA WITH SARDINES (AND WILD FENNEL), 69
PASTA WITH SEA-URCHINS, 68
PASTA WITH SICILIAN-STYLE "PESTO", 65
PASTA WITH SWORDFISH AND MINT, 65
SICILIAN BROCCOLI AND PASTA SOUP, 50
SICILIAN PASTA TIMBALE, 76
SICILIAN-STYLE STUFFED CANNELLONI, 49
SPAGHETTI WITH A PIQUANT SAUCE, 58
SPAGHETTI WITH CLAMS, 72
SPAGHETTI WITH MUSSELS, 60
SPAGHETTI WITH TUNA ROE, 58
TRAPANI-STYLE PASTA, 71

MEAT DISHES

BAKED PORK SHINS, 107
BEEF STEW WITH POTATOES, 104
BOILED BEEF, 94
BREADED HEART, 86
BREADED PORK STEAKS, 85
CALF GRISTLE SALAD, 91
CHICKEN DRUMSTICKS, 89
CHICKEN WITH TOMATOES, 96
"CONCA D'ORO" ESCALOPES, 101
FRIED MEATBALLS, 97
GRILLED LAMB CUTLETS, 84
GRILLED MIXED KEBABS, 106
KID MEAT STEW WITH POTATOES, 103
LEMON ESCALOPES, 102
MARSALA ESCALOPES, 102
MEAT AND CITRON KEBABS, 105
MEAT LOAF, 99
MEATBALLS IN SAUCE, 98
MIXED PORK MEAT IN SAUCE, 95
OLIVETAN-STYLE TRIPE, 108

PALERMO-STYLE LIVER, 88
PALERMO-STYLE SAUSAGES, 100
PALERMO-STYLE STEAK, 80
PALERMO-STYLE TOP ROUND, 90
PORK CHOPS WITH BLACK OLIVES, 85
RABBIT IN RED WINE, 83
ROAST LAMB, 78
ROULADES IN SAUCE, 93
ROULADES, 92
SAUSAGES IN WHITE WINE, 100
STEAK IN A VINEGAR AND OREGANO DRESSING, 79
STEWED LAMB, 78
STEWED RABBIT, 82
STUFFED MEAT ROLL, 87
SWEET AND SOUR LIVER, 88
SWEET AND SOUR RABBIT WITH GREEN OLIVES AND
     CAPERS, 82
SWEET AND SOUR RABBIT, 85
VEAL STEAKS, 81

Thanks

If it is true that in producing this book enthusiasm, patience and precision have been my most trusted collaborators, I feel I really must express my warmest thanks to all those who in their various ways have made this publication possible.

Chef Francesco Paolo Gnizio from the "A Cuccagna" restaurant, my brother-in-law Vito Alba at the Cafè Royal (confectionery), my mother, my wife and my sister Anna, the cake-maker of the family.

And finally my most heartfelt thanks go to Professor Elda Joly and architect Rodo Santoro for the introduction and the ink drawings.

Carmelo Sammarco

Printed in January 2001
by Luxograph s.r.l. - Palermo